FOREWORD

The collection of "Everything Will Be Okay" travel phrasebooks published by T&P Books is designed for people traveling abroad for tourism and business. The phrasebooks contain what matters most - the essentials for basic communication. This is an indispensable set of phrases to "survive" while abroad.

This phrasebook will help you in most cases where you need to ask something, get directions, find out how much something costs, etc. It can also resolve difficult communication situations where gestures just won't help.

This book contains a lot of phrases that have been grouped according to the most relevant topics. A separate section of the book also provides a small dictionary with more than 1,500 important and useful words.

Take "Everything Will Be Okay" phrasebook with you on the road and you'll have an irreplaceable traveling companion who will help you find your way out of any situation and teach you to not fear speaking with foreigners.

TABLE OF CONTENTS

T&P Books Publishing

T&P Books Publishing

PHRASEBOOK

— DANISH —

THE MOST IMPORTANT PHRASES

This phrasebook contains
the most important
phrases and questions
for basic communication
Everything you need
to survive overseas

By Andrey Taranov

T&P BOOKS

Phrasebook + 1500-word dictionary

English-Danish phrasebook & concise dictionary

By Andrey Taranov

The collection of "Everything Will Be Okay" travel phrasebooks published by T&P Books is designed for people traveling abroad for tourism and business. The phrasebooks contain what matters most - the essentials for basic communication. This is an indispensable set of phrases to "survive" while abroad.

Another section of the book also provides a small dictionary with more than 1,500 useful words arranged alphabetically. The dictionary includes a lot of gastronomic terms and will be helpful when ordering food at a restaurant or buying groceries at the store.

T&P Books Publishing
www.tpbooks.com

ISBN: 978-1-78492-445-4

This book is also available in E-book formats.
Please visit www.tpbooks.com or the major online bookstores.

PRONUNCIATION

Letter	Danish example	T&P phonetic alphabet	English example
Aa	Afrika, kompas	[æ], [ɑ], [ɑ:]	man, father
Bb	barberblad	[b]	baby, book
Cc	cafe, creme	[k]	clock, kiss
Cc [1]	koncert	[s]	city, boss
Dd	direktør	[d]	day, doctor
Dd [2]	facade	[ð]	weather, together
Ee	belgier	[e], [ə]	medal, elm
Ee [3]	elevator	[ɛ]	man, bad
Ff	familie	[f]	face, food
Gg	mango	[g]	game, gold
Hh	høne, knurhår	[h]	home, have
Ii	kolibri	[i], [i:]	feet, Peter
Jj	legetøj	[j]	yes, New York
Kk	leksikon	[k]	clock, kiss
Ll	leopard	[l]	lace, people
Mm	marmor	[m]	magic, milk
Nn	natur, navn	[n]	name, normal
ng	omfang	[ŋ]	English, ring
nk	punktum	[ŋ]	English, ring
Oo	fortov	[o], [ɔ]	drop, baught
Pp	planteolie	[p]	pencil, private
Qq	sequoia	[k]	clock, kiss
Rr	seriøs	[ʁ]	French (guttural) R
Ss	selskab	[s]	city, boss
Tt	strøm, trappe	[t]	tourist, trip
Uu	blæksprutte	[u:]	pool, room
Vv	børnehave	[ʊ]	vase, winter
Ww	whisky	[w]	vase, winter
Xx	Luxembourg	[ks]	box, taxi
Yy	lykke	[y], [ø]	fuel, eternal
Zz	Venezuela	[s]	city, boss

Letter	Danish example	T&P phonetic alphabet	English example
Ææ	ærter	[ɛ], [ɛ:]	habit, bad
Øø	grønsager	[ø], [œ]	church, eternal
Åå	åbent, afgå	[ɔ], [o:]	sun, lucky

Comments

[1] before **e, i**
[2] after a stressed vowel
[3] at the beginning of words

LIST OF ABBREVIATIONS

English abbreviations

ab.	-	about
adj	-	adjective
adv	-	adverb
anim.	-	animate
as adj	-	attributive noun used as adjective
e.g.	-	for example
etc.	-	et cetera
fam.	-	familiar
fem.	-	feminine
form.	-	formal
inanim.	-	inanimate
masc.	-	masculine
math	-	mathematics
mil.	-	military
n	-	noun
pl	-	plural
pron.	-	pronoun
sb	-	somebody
sing.	-	singular
sth	-	something
v aux	-	auxiliary verb
vi	-	intransitive verb
vi, vt	-	intransitive, transitive verb
vt	-	transitive verb

Danish abbreviations

f	-	common gender
f pl	-	common gender plural
i	-	neuter
i pl	-	neuter plural
i, f	-	neuter, common gender
ngn.	-	somebody
pl	-	plural

T&P BOOKS

DANISH PHRASEBOOK

This section contains
important phrases that may
come in handy in various
real-life situations.
The phrasebook will help
you ask for directions, clarify
a price, buy tickets, and
order food at a restaurant

T&P Books Publishing

PHRASEBOOK
CONTENTS

The bare minimum

Excuse me, ...

Undskyld, ...
['ɔn̩ˌskyl̩', ...]

Hello.

Hej.
['hɑj]

Thank you.

Tak.
[tɑk]

Good bye.

Farvel.
[fɑ'vɛl]

Yes.

Ja.
['jæ]

No.

Nej.
[nɑj']

I don't know.

Jeg ved det ikke.
[jɑj ve de 'ekə]

Where? | Where to? | When?

Hvor? | Hvorhen? | Hvornår?
['vɒ'? | 'vɒ'ˌhɛn? | vɒ'nɒ'?]

I need ...

Jeg har brug for ...
[jɑ hɑ' 'bʁu' fə ...]

I want ...

Jeg vil ...
[jɑj ve ...]

Do you have ...?

Har du ...?
['hɑ' du ...?]

Is there a ... here?

Er der en ... her?
[æɐ̯ 'dɛ'ɐ̯ en ... hɛ'ɐ̯?]

May I ...?

Må jeg ...?
[mɔ' jɑ ...?]

..., please (polite request)

... venligst
[... 'vɛnlist]

I'm looking for ...

Jeg leder efter ...
[jɑ 'le:ðə 'ɛftʌ ...]

restroom

toilet
[toa'lɛt]

ATM

udbetalingsautomat
[uð'be'tæ'leŋs ɑwto'mæ't]

pharmacy (drugstore)

apotek
[ɑpo'te'k]

hospital

hospital
[hɔspi'tæ'l]

police station

politistation
[poli'ti sta'ɕo'n]

subway

metro
['me:tʁo]

taxi	**taxi** ['tɑksi]
train station	**togstation** ['tɔw stɑ'ɕoˀn]

My name is ...	**Mit navn er ...** [mit 'nɑwˀn 'æɐ̯ ...]
What's your name?	**Hvad er dit navn?** ['vað 'æɐ̯ dit nɑwˀn?]
Could you please help me?	**Kan du hjælpe mig?** ['kan du 'jɛlpə mɑj?]
I've got a problem.	**Jeg har fået et problem.** [jɑ hɑˀ fɔˀ et pʁoˈbleˀm]
I don't feel well.	**Jeg føler mig dårlig.** [jɑ 'føːlɐ mɑj 'dɒːli]
Call an ambulance!	**Ring efter en ambulance!** ['ʁɛŋə 'ɛftʌ en ɑmbu'lɑŋsə]
May I make a call?	**Må jeg foretage et opkald?** [mɔˀ jɑ 'fɔːɒˌtæˀ et 'ʌpkalˀ?]

I'm sorry.	**Det er jeg ked af.** [de 'æɐ̯ jɑ 'keðˀ æˀ]
You're welcome.	**Selv tak.** [sɛlˀ tak]

I, me	**Jeg, mig** [jɑj, mɑj]
you (inform.)	**du** [du]
he	**han** [han]
she	**hun** [hun]
they (masc.)	**de** [di]
they (fem.)	**de** [di]
we	**vi** [vi]
you (pl)	**I, De** [I, di]
you (sg, form.)	**De** [di]

ENTRANCE	**INDGANG** ['enˌgɑŋˀ]
EXIT	**UDGANG** ['uðˌgɑŋˀ]
OUT OF ORDER	**UDE AF DRIFT** ['uːðə æˀ 'dʁɛft]
CLOSED	**LUKKET** ['lokəð]

OPEN	**ÅBEN**
	['ɔ:bən]
FOR WOMEN	**TIL KVINDER**
	[te 'kvenʌ]
FOR MEN	**TIL MÆND**
	[te 'mɛnˀ]

Questions

Where?	**Hvor?** ['vɒˀ?]
Where to?	**Hvorhen?** ['vɒˀˌhɛn?]
Where from?	**Hvorfra?** ['vɒˀˌfʁɑˀ?]
Why?	**Hvorfor?** ['vɔfʌ?]
For what reason?	**Af hvilken grund?** [æˀ 'velkən 'gʁɔnˀ?]
When?	**Hvornår?** [vɒ'nɒˀ?]

How long?	**Hvor længe?** [vɒˀ 'lɛŋə?]
At what time?	**På hvilket tidspunkt?** [pɔ 'velkəð 'tiðspɒŋˀt?]
How much?	**Hvor meget?** [vɒˀ 'mɑɑð?]
Do you have ...?	**Har du ...?** ['hɑˀ du ...?]
Where is ...?	**Hvor er ...?** [vɒˀ 'æɐ̯ ...?]

What time is it?	**Hvad er klokken?** ['vað 'æɐ̯ 'klʌkən?]
May I make a call?	**Må jeg foretage et opkald?** [mɔˀ jɑ 'fɒːɒˌtæˀ et 'ʌpkalˀ?]
Who's there?	**Hvem der?** [vɛm 'dɛˀɐ̯?]
Can I smoke here?	**Må jeg ryge her?** [mɔˀ jɑ 'ʁyːə 'hɛˀɐ̯?]
May I ...?	**Må jeg ...?** [mɔˀ jɑ ...?]

Needs

I'd like ...	**Jeg vil gerne ...** [jɑj ve 'gæɐ̯nə ...]
I don't want ...	**Jeg ønsker ikke ...** [jɑ 'ønskɐ 'ekə ...]
I'm thirsty.	**Jeg er tørstig.** ['jɑj 'æɐ̯ 'tœɐ̯sti]
I want to sleep.	**Jeg ønsker at sove.** [jɑ 'ønskɐ ʌ 'sɒwə]

I want ...	**Jeg vil ...** [jɑj ve ...]
to wash up	**at vaske** [ʌ 'vaskə]
to brush my teeth	**at børste mine tænder** [ʌ 'bœɐ̯stə 'miːnə 'tɛnʌ]
to rest a while	**at hvile en stund** [ʌ 'viːlə en 'stonʔ]
to change my clothes	**at klæde mig om** [ʌ 'klɛʔ 'mɑj ʌm]

to go back to the hotel	**at gå tilbage til hotellet** [ʌ 'gɔʔ te'bæːjə te ho'tɛlʔəð]
to buy ...	**at købe ...** [ʌ 'køːbə ...]
to go to ...	**at gå til ...** [ʌ 'gɔ te ...]
to visit ...	**at besøge ...** [ʌ be'søʔjə ...]
to meet with ...	**at mødes med ...** [ʌ 'møːðəs mɛ ...]
to make a call	**at foretage et opkald** [ʌ 'fɒːɒˌtæʔ et 'ʌpkalʔ]

I'm tired.	**Jeg er træt.** ['jɑj 'æɐ̯ 'tʁat]
We are tired.	**Vi er trætte.** ['vi 'æɐ̯ 'tʁatə]
I'm cold.	**Jeg fryser.** [jɑ 'fʁyːsʌ]
I'm hot.	**Jeg har det varmt.** [jɑ haʔ de 'vɑʔmt]
I'm OK.	**Jeg er OK.** ['jɑj 'æɐ̯ ɔw'kɛj]

I need to make a call.	**Jeg har brug for at foretage et opkald.** [ja haˀ 'bʁuˀ fə ʌ 'foːɒˌtæˀ et ˈʌpkalˀ]
I need to go to the restroom.	**Jeg har brug for at gå på toilettet.** [ja haˀ 'bʁuˀ fə ʌ gɔˀ pɔ toaˈlɛət]
I have to go.	**Jeg er nødt til at gå.** ['jaj 'æɛ̯ nøˀt te ʌ gɔˀ]
I have to go now.	**Jeg er nødt til at gå nu.** ['jaj 'æɛ̯ nøˀt te ʌ gɔˀ nu]

Asking for directions

Excuse me, ...	**Undskyld, ...** ['ɔnˌskyl', ...]
Where is ...?	**Hvor er ...?** [vɒ' 'æɐ̯ ...?]
Which way is ...?	**Hvilken vej er ...?** ['velkən 'vɑj' 'æɐ̯ ...?]
Could you help me, please?	**Er du sød at hjælpe mig?** [æɐ̯ du 'søð' ʌ 'jɛlpə mɑj?]
I'm looking for ...	**Jeg leder efter ...** [ja 'le:ðə 'ɛftʌ ...]
I'm looking for the exit.	**Jeg leder efter udgangen.** [ja 'le:ðə 'ɛftʌ 'uðˌgɑŋən]
I'm going to ...	**Jeg har tænkt mig at ...** [ja hɑ' 'tɛŋkt mɑj ʌ ...]
Am I going the right way to ...?	**Går jeg den rigtige vej til ...?** [gɒ' ja dən 'ʁɛgtiə vɑj' te ...?]
Is it far?	**Er det langt væk?** [æɐ̯ de 'lɑŋ't vɛk?]
Can I get there on foot?	**Kan jeg komme derhen til fods?** ['kan' ja 'kʌmə 'dɛ'ɐ̯'hɛn te 'fo'ðs?]
Can you show me on the map?	**Kan du vise mig på kortet?** ['kan du 'vi:sə mɑj pɔ 'kɒ:təð?]
Show me where we are right now.	**Vis mig, hvor vi er lige nu.** ['vi's mɑj, vɒ' vi 'æɐ̯ 'li:ə nu]
Here	**Her** ['hɛ'ɐ̯]
There	**Der** [dɛ'ɐ̯]
This way	**Denne vej** ['dɛnə vɑj']
Turn right.	**Drej til højre.** [dʁɑj' te 'hʌjʁʌ]
Turn left.	**Drej til venstre.** [dʁɑj' te 'vɛnstʁʌ]
first (second, third) turn	**første (anden, tredje) vej** ['fœɐ̯stə ('anən, 'tʁɛðjə) vɑj']
to the right	**til højre** [te 'hʌjʁʌ]

to the left

til venstre
[te 'vɛnstʁʌ]

Go straight ahead.

Gå ligeud.
['gɔˀ 'liːə'uðˀ]

Signs

WELCOME!	**VELKOMMEN!** ['vɛlˌkʌmˀən]
ENTRANCE	**INDGANG** ['enˌgɑŋˀ]
EXIT	**UDGANG** ['uðˌgɑŋˀ]
PUSH	**SKUB** [skɔb]
PULL	**TRÆK** ['tʁak]
OPEN	**ÅBEN** ['ɔ:bən]
CLOSED	**LUKKET** ['lɔkəð]
FOR WOMEN	**TIL KVINDER** [te 'kvenʌ]
FOR MEN	**TIL MÆND** [te 'mɛnˀ]
GENTLEMEN, GENTS (m)	**MÆND** [mɛnˀ]
WOMEN (f)	**KVINDER** ['kvenʌ]
DISCOUNTS	**UDSALG** ['uðˌsalˀ]
SALE	**RESTSALG** ['ʁast ˌsalˀ]
FREE	**GRATIS** ['gʁɑ:tis]
NEW!	**NYT!** [nyt]
ATTENTION!	**OBS!** [ʌbs]
NO VACANCIES	**ALT OPTAGET** ['alˀt 'ʌpˌtæˀəð]
RESERVED	**RESERVERET** [ʁɛsæɐ̯'veˀʌð]
ADMINISTRATION	**ADMINISTRATION** [aðministʁɑ'ɕoˀn]
STAFF ONLY	**KUN PERSONALE** [kɔn pæɐ̯so'næ:lə]

BEWARE OF THE DOG! **PAS PÅ HUNDEN!**
[pas pɔ 'hunən]

NO SMOKING! **RYGNING FORBUDT!**
['ʁy:nen fʌ'byˀd]

DO NOT TOUCH! **RØR IKKE!**
['ʁœˀɐ 'ekə]

DANGEROUS **FARLIGT**
['fɑ:lit]

DANGER **FARE**
['fɑ:ɑ]

HIGH VOLTAGE **STÆRKSTRØM**
['stæɐk 'stʁœmˀ]

NO SWIMMING! **SVØMNING FORBUDT!**
['svœmnen fʌ'byˀt]

OUT OF ORDER **UDE AF DRIFT**
['u:ðə æˀ 'dʁɛft]

FLAMMABLE **BRANDFARLIG**
['bʁɑn‚fɑ:li]

FORBIDDEN **FORBUDT**
[fʌ'byˀt]

NO TRESPASSING! **ADGANG FORBUDT!**
['að‚gɑŋˀ fʌ'byˀð]

WET PAINT **VÅD MALING**
['vɔˀð 'mæ:len]

CLOSED FOR RENOVATIONS **LUKKET PGA. RENOVERING**
['lokəð pɔˀ 'gʁɔnˀ a ʁɛno've'ɐen]

WORKS AHEAD **ARBEJDE FORUDE**
['ɑ:‚bɑjˀdə 'fɔ:‚u:ðə]

DETOUR **OMKØRSEL**
[ɔm'køɐsəl]

Transportation. General phrases

plane	**fly** [fly']
train	**tog** ['tɔ'w]
bus	**bus** [bus]
ferry	**færge** ['fæɐ̯wə]
taxi	**taxi** ['tɑksi]
car	**bil** [bi'l]

schedule	**køreplan** ['kø:ʌˌplæ'n]
Where can I see the schedule?	**Hvor kan jeg se køreplanen?** [vɒ' kan jɑ se' 'kø:ʌˌplæ'nən?]
workdays (weekdays)	**hverdage** ['væɐ̯ˌdæ'ə]
weekends	**weekender** ['wi:ˌkɛndʌ]
holidays	**helligdage** ['hɛliˌdæ'ə]

DEPARTURE	**AFGANG** ['ɑwˌgɑŋ']
ARRIVAL	**ANKOMST** ['anˌkʌm'st]
DELAYED	**FORSINKET** [fə'seŋ'kəð]
CANCELLED	**AFLYST** ['ɑwˌly'st]

next (train, etc.)	**næste** ['nɛstə]
first	**første** ['fœɐ̯stə]
last	**sidste** ['sistə]

When is the next ...?	**Hvornår er den næste ...?** [vɒ'nɒ' 'æɐ̯ dən 'nɛstə ...?]
When is the first ...?	**Hvornår er den første ...?** [vɒ'nɒ' 'æɐ̯ dən 'fœɐ̯stə ...?]

When is the last ...? **Hvornår er den sidste ...?**
[vɒˈnɒˀ ˈæɡ dən ˈsistə ...?]

transfer (change of trains, etc.) **skift**
[ˈskift]

to make a transfer **at skifte**
[ʌ ˈskiftə]

Do I need to make a transfer? **Behøver jeg at skifte?**
[beˈhøˀvə ˈjɑj ʌ ˈskiftə?]

Buying tickets

Where can I buy tickets?	**Hvor kan jeg købe billetter?** [vɒˀ kan jɑ ˈkøːbə biˈlɛtʌ?]
ticket	**billet** [biˈlɛt]
to buy a ticket	**at købe en billet** [ʌ ˈkøːbə en biˈlɛt]
ticket price	**billetpris** [biˈlɛtˌpʁiˀs]

Where to?	**Hvorhen?** [ˈvɒˀˌhɛn?]
To what station?	**Til hvilken station?** [te ˈvelkən staˈɕoˀn?]
I need ...	**Jeg har brug for ...** [jɑ haˀ ˈbʁuˀ fə ...]
one ticket	**én billet** [en biˈlɛt]
two tickets	**to billetter** [toˀ biˈlɛtʌ]
three tickets	**tre billetter** [ˈtʁɛˀ biˈlɛtʌ]

one-way	**enkelt** [ˈɛŋˀkəlt]
round-trip	**retur** [ʁɛˈtuʁˀ]
first class	**første klasse** [ˈfœʁstə ˈklasə]
second class	**anden klasse** [ˈanən ˈklasə]

today	**i dag** [i ˈdæˀ]
tomorrow	**i morgen** [i ˈmɒːɒn]
the day after tomorrow	**i overmorgen** [i ˈɒwʌˌmɒːɒn]
in the morning	**om morgenen** [ʌm ˈmɒːɒnən]
in the afternoon	**om eftermiddagen** [ʌm ˈɛftʌmeˌdæˀən]
in the evening	**om aftenen** [ʌm ˈɑftənən]

aisle seat

gangplads
['gɑŋplas]

window seat

vinduesplads
['vendus 'plas]

How much?

Hvor meget?
[vɒˀ 'mɑɑð?]

Can I pay by credit card?

Kan jeg betale med kreditkort?
['kanˀ jɑ be'tæˀlə mɛ kʁɛ'dit kɒ:t?]

Bus

bus	**bus** [bus]
intercity bus	**rutebil** ['ʁuːtəˌbiʔl]
bus stop	**busstoppested** ['busˌstɔpəstɛð]
Where's the nearest bus stop?	**Hvor er det nærmeste busstoppested?** [vɒˀ 'æɐ̯ de 'næɐ̯məstə 'busˌstɔpəstɛð?]
number (bus ~, etc.)	**nummer** ['nɔmˀʌ]
Which bus do I take to get to …?	**Hvilken bus skal jeg tage for at komme til …?** ['velkən bus skalˀ jɑ 'tæˀə fə ʌ 'kʌmə te …?]
Does this bus go to …?	**Kører denne bus til …?** ['køːɐ̯ 'dɛnə bus te …?]
How frequent are the buses?	**Hvor hyppigt kører busserne?** [vɒˀ 'hypit 'køːɐ̯ 'busɐnə?]
every 15 minutes	**hvert kvarter** ['vɛˀɐ̯t kvɑ'teˀɐ̯]
every half hour	**hver halve time** ['vɛɐ̯ halˀvə 'tiːmə]
every hour	**hver time** ['vɛɐ̯ 'tiːmə]
several times a day	**flere gange om dagen** ['fleːʌ 'gɑŋə ʌm 'dæˀən]
… times a day	**… gange om dagen** [… 'gɑŋə ʌm 'dæˀən]
schedule	**køreplan** ['køːʌˌplæˀn]
Where can I see the schedule?	**Hvor kan jeg se køreplanen?** [vɒˀ kan jɑ seˀ 'køːʌˌplæˀnən?]
When is the next bus?	**Hvornår kører den næste bus?** [vɒ'nɒˀ 'køːɐ̯ dən 'nɛstə bus?]
When is the first bus?	**Hvornår kører den første bus?** [vɒ'nɒˀ 'køːɐ̯ dən 'fœɐ̯stə bus?]
When is the last bus?	**Hvornår kører den sidste bus?** [vɒ'nɒˀ 'køːɐ̯ dən 'sistə bus?]

stop

stop
['stʌp]

next stop

næste stop
['nɛstə 'stʌp]

last stop (terminus)

sidste stop
['sistə 'stʌp]

Stop here, please.

Stop her, tak.
['stʌp 'hɛˀɐ̯, tɑk]

Excuse me, this is my stop.

Undskyld, det er mit stop.
['ɔnˌskylˀ, de 'æɐ̯ mit 'stʌp]

Train

train	**tog** ['tɔˀw]
suburban train	**regionaltog** [ʁɛgjoˈnæˀl tɔˀw]
long-distance train	**intercitytog** [entʌˈsiti tɔˀw]
train station	**togstation** ['tɔw staˈɕoˀn]
Excuse me, where is the exit to the platform?	**Undskyld, hvor er udgangen til perronen?** ['ɔnˌskylˀ, vɒˀ 'æɐ̯ 'uðˌgɑŋən te paˈʁʌŋən?]

Does this train go to ...?	**Kører dette tog til ...?** ['køːɐ̯ 'dɛtə tɔˀw te ...?]
next train	**næste tog** ['nɛstə 'tɔˀw]
When is the next train?	**Hvornår afgår det næste tog?** [vɒˈnɒˀ 'awˌgɒˀ de 'nɛstə tɔˀw?]
Where can I see the schedule?	**Hvor kan jeg se køreplanen?** [vɒˀ kan ja seˀ 'køːʌˌplæˀnən?]
From which platform?	**Fra hvilken perron?** [ˌfʁaˀ 'velkən paˈʁʌŋ?]
When does the train arrive in ...?	**Hvornår ankommer toget til ...?** [vɒˈnɒˀ 'anˌkʌmʌ 'tɔˀwəð te ...?]

Please help me.	**Vær sød at hjælpe mig.** ['vɛɐ̯ˀ 'søðˀ ʌ 'jɛlpə maj]
I'm looking for my seat.	**Jeg leder efter min plads.** [ja 'leːðə 'ɛftʌ min plas]
We're looking for our seats.	**Vi leder efter vores pladser.** ['vi 'leːðə 'ɛftʌ 'vɒɒs 'plasʌ]
My seat is taken.	**Min plads er taget.** [min 'plas 'æɐ̯ 'tæəð]
Our seats are taken.	**Vore pladser er taget.** ['vɒːɒ 'plasʌ 'æɐ̯ 'tæəð]

I'm sorry but this is my seat.	**Jeg beklager, men dette er min plads.** [ja beˈklæˀjə, mɛn 'dɛtə 'æɐ̯ min 'plas]
Is this seat taken?	**Er denne plads taget?** [æɐ̯ 'dɛnə plas 'tæəð?]
May I sit here?	**Må jeg sidde her?** [mɔˀ ja 'seðə 'hɛˀɐ̯?]

On the train. Dialogue (No ticket)

Ticket, please.

Billet, tak.
[bi'lɛt, tak]

I don't have a ticket.

Jeg har ikke nogen billet.
[ja haʔ 'ekə 'noən bi'lɛt]

I lost my ticket.

Jeg har mistet min billet.
[ja haʔ 'mestəð min bi'lɛt]

I forgot my ticket at home.

Jeg har glemt min billet derhjemme.
[ja haʔ 'glɛmt min bi'lɛt da'jɛmə]

You can buy a ticket from me.

Du kan købe en billet af mig.
[du kan 'køːbə en bi'lɛt æʔ maj]

You will also have to pay a fine.

**Du bliver også nødt
til at betale en bøde.**
[du 'bliɐ̯ʔ 'ʌsə nøʔt
te ʌ be'tæʔlə en 'bøːðə]

Okay.

OK.
[ɔw'kɛj]

Where are you going?

Hvor skal du hen?
[vɒʔ skalʔ du hɛn?]

I'm going to ...

Jeg har tænkt mig at ...
[ja haʔ 'tɛŋkt maj ʌ ...]

How much? I don't understand.

Hvor meget? Jeg forstår det ikke.
[vɒʔ 'maað? ja fə'stǫ̊ de 'ekə]

Write it down, please.

Skriv det ned, tak.
['skʁiwʔ de neð', tak]

Okay. Can I pay with a credit card?

OK. Kan jeg betale med kreditkort?
[ɔw'kɛj. kan ja be'tæʔlə mɛ kʁɛ'dit kɒːt?]

Yes, you can.

Ja, det kan du godt.
['jæ, de kan du 'gʌt]

Here's your receipt.

Her er din kvittering.
['hɛʔɐ̯ 'æɐ̯ din kvi'teʔɐ̯eŋ]

Sorry about the fine.

Undskyld bøden.
['ɔnˌskylʔ 'bøːðən]

That's okay. It was my fault.

Det er OK. Det var min skyld.
[de 'æɐ̯ ɔw'kɛj. de va min skylʔ]

Enjoy your trip.

Nyd turen.
[nyð 'tuɐ̯ʔn]

Taxi

taxi	**taxi** ['tɑksi]
taxi driver	**taxichauffør** ['tɑksi ɕo'fø'ɐ̯]
to catch a taxi	**at få fat i en taxi** [ʌ fɔ' fat i en 'tɑksi]
taxi stand	**taxiholdeplads** ['tɑksi 'hʌlə‚plas]
Where can I get a taxi?	**Hvor kan jeg finde en taxi?** [vɒ' kan jɑj 'fenə en 'tɑksi?]
to call a taxi	**at ringe efter en taxi** [ʌ 'ʁɛŋə 'ɛftʌ en 'tɑksi]
I need a taxi.	**Jeg har brug for en taxi.** [jɑ hɑ' 'bʁu' fə en 'tɑksi]
Right now.	**Lige nu.** ['liːə 'nu]
What is your address (location)?	**Hvad er din adresse?** ['vað 'æɐ̯ din a'dʁasə?]
My address is ...	**Min adresse er ...** [min a'dʁasə 'æɐ̯ ...]
Your destination?	**Hvor skal du hen?** [vɒ' skal' du hɛn?]
Excuse me, ...	**Undskyld, ...** ['ɔn‚skyl', ...]
Are you available?	**Er du ledig?** [æɐ̯ du 'leːði?]
How much is it to get to ...?	**Hvor meget koster det at komme til ...?** [vɒ' 'maɑð 'kʌstɐ̯ de ʌ 'kʌmə te ...?]
Do you know where it is?	**Ved du, hvor det er?** [ve du, vɒ' de 'æɐ̯?]
Airport, please.	**Lufthavnen, tak.** ['lɔft‚haw'nən, tɑk]
Stop here, please.	**Stop her, tak.** ['stʌp 'hɛ'ɐ̯, tɑk]
It's not here.	**Det er ikke her.** [de 'æɐ̯ 'ekə 'hɛ'ɐ̯]
This is the wrong address.	**Det er den forkerte adresse.** [de 'æɐ̯ dən fə'keɐ̯'tə a'dʁasə]

Turn left.

Drej til venstre.
[dʁɑjˀ te ˈvɛnstʁʌ]

Turn right.

Drej til højre.
[dʁɑjˀ te ˈhʌjʁʌ]

How much do I owe you?

Hvor meget skylder jeg dig?
[vɒˀ ˈmɑɑð ˈskylə jɑ dɑjˀ]

I'd like a receipt, please.

Jeg vil gerne have en kvittering, tak.
[jɑj ve ˈgæɐ̯nə hæˀ en kviˈteˀɐ̯eŋ, tɑk]

Keep the change.

Behold resten.
[beˈhʌlˀ ˈʁastən]

Would you please wait for me?

Vil du venligst vente på mig?
[ˈve du ˈvɛnlist ˈvɛntə pɔ mɑj?]

five minutes

fem minutter
[fɛmˀ meˈnutʌ]

ten minutes

ti minutter
[ˈtiˀ meˈnutʌ]

fifteen minutes

femten minutter
[ˈfɛmtən meˈnutʌ]

twenty minutes

tyve minutter
[ˈtyːvə meˈnutʌ]

half an hour

en halv time
[en ˈhalˀ ˈtiːmə]

Hotel

Hello.	**Hej.** ['hɑj]
My name is …	**Mit navn er …** [mit 'nɑwʔn 'æɐ̯ …]
I have a reservation.	**Jeg har en reservation.** [jɑ hɑʔ en ʁɛsæɐ̯va'ɕoʔn]
I need …	**Jeg har brug for …** [jɑ hɑʔ 'bʁuʔ fə …]
a single room	**et enkeltværelse** [et 'ɛŋʔkəlt̩ˌvæɐ̯ʌlsə]
a double room	**et dobbeltværelse** [et 'dʌbəlt 'væɐ̯ʌlsə]
How much is that?	**Hvor meget bliver det?** [vɒʔ 'mɑɑð 'bliɐ̯ʔ de?]
That's a bit expensive.	**Det er lidt dyrt.** [de 'æɐ̯ lit 'dyɐ̯ʔt]
Do you have anything else?	**Har du nogen andre muligheder?** ['hɑʔ du 'noən 'ɑndʁʌ 'muːliˌheðʔʌ?]
I'll take it.	**Det tager jeg.** [de 'tæʔɐ̯ jɑj]
I'll pay in cash.	**Jeg betaler kontant.** [jɑ be'tæʔlʌ kɔn'tanʔt]
I've got a problem.	**Jeg har fået et problem.** [jɑ hɑʔ fɔʔ et pʁo'bleʔm]
My … is broken.	**Mit … er gået i stykker.** [mit … 'æɐ̯ 'gɔːəð 'støkʌ]
My … is out of order.	**Mit … virker ikke.** [mit … 'viɐ̯kʌ 'ekə]
TV	**TV** ['teʔˌveʔ]
air conditioner	**klimaanlæg** ['kliːma'anˌlɛʔg]
tap	**hane** ['hæːnə]
shower	**bruser** ['bʁuːsʌ]
sink	**vask** ['vask]
safe	**pengeskab** ['pɛŋəˌskæʔb]

door lock	**dørlås** ['dœɐ̯lɔˀs]
electrical outlet	**stikkontakt** ['stek kɔn'tɑkt]
hairdryer	**hårtørrer** ['hɔːˌtœɐ̯ʌ]

I don't have ...	**Jeg har ikke nogen ...** [jɑ hɑˀ 'ekə 'noən ...]
water	**vand** ['vanˀ]
light	**lys** ['lyˀs]
electricity	**elektricitet** [elɛktʁisi'teˀt]

Can you give me ...?	**Kan du give mig ...?** ['kan du giˀ mɑj ...?]
a towel	**et håndklæde** [ed 'hʌnˌklɛːðə]
a blanket	**et tæppe** [ed 'tɛpə]
slippers	**hjemmesko** ['jɛməˌskoˀ]
a robe	**en kåbe** [en 'kɔːbə]
shampoo	**shampoo** ['ɕæːmˌpuː]
soap	**sæbe** ['sɛːbə]

I'd like to change rooms.	**Jeg vil gerne skifte værelse.** [jɑj ve 'gæɐ̯nə 'skiftə 'væɐ̯ʌlsə]
I can't find my key.	**Jeg kan ikke finde min nøgle.** [jɑ kan 'ekə 'fenə min 'nʌjlə]
Could you open my room, please?	**Kunne du låse op til mit værelse?** ['kunə du 'lɔːsə ʌp te mit 'væɐ̯ʌlsə?]
Who's there?	**Hvem der?** [vɛm 'dɛˀɐ̯?]
Come in!	**Kom ind!** [kʌmˀ enˀ]
Just a minute!	**Et øjeblik!** [ed 'ʌjə'blek]
Not right now, please.	**Ikke lige nu, tak.** ['ekə 'liːə nu, tɑk]

Come to my room, please.	**Kom til mit værelse, tak.** [kʌmˀ te mit 'væɐ̯ʌlsə, tɑk]
I'd like to order food service.	**Jeg vil gerne bestille roomservice.** [jɑj ve 'gæɐ̯nə be'stelˀə 'ʁuːmˌsœːvis]
My room number is ...	**Mit værelsesnummer er ...** [mit 'væɐ̯ʌlsə'nɔmˀʌ 'æɐ̯ ...]

I'm leaving …	**Jeg forlader …** [ja fə'læ'ðə …]
We're leaving …	**Vi forlader …** ['vi fə'læ'ðə …]
right now	**lige nu** ['liːə 'nu]
this afternoon	**i eftermiddag** [I 'ɛftʌmeˌdæ']
tonight	**i aften** [i 'aftən]
tomorrow	**i morgen** [i 'mɒːɒn]
tomorrow morning	**i morgen tidlig** [i 'mɒːɒn 'tiðli]
tomorrow evening	**i morgen aften** [i 'mɒːɒn 'aftən]
the day after tomorrow	**i overmorgen** [i 'ɒwʌˌmɒːɒn]

I'd like to pay.	**Jeg vil gerne betale.** [jaj ve 'gæɐ̯nə be'tæ'lə]
Everything was wonderful.	**Alt var vidunderligt.** ['al't va við'ɔn'ʌlit]
Where can I get a taxi?	**Hvor kan jeg finde en taxi?** [vɒ' kan jaj 'fenə en 'taksi?]
Would you call a taxi for me, please?	**Vil du ringe efter en taxi for mig, tak?** ['ve du 'ʁɛŋə 'ɛftʌ en 'taksi fə maj, tak?]

Restaurant

Can I look at the menu, please?

Kan jeg se menuen?
['kan' ja se' me'nyən?]

Table for one.

Bord til én.
['bo'ɐ̯ te 'en]

There are two (three, four) of us.

Vi er to (tre, fire).
[vi 'æɐ̯ to' ('tʁɛ', 'fi'ʌ)]

Smoking

Rygning
['ʁy:neŋ]

No smoking

Rygning forbudt
['ʁy:neŋ fʌ'by'd]

Excuse me! (addressing a waiter)

Undskyld!
['ɔn,skyl']

menu

menu
[me'ny]

wine list

vinkort
['vi:n,kɒ:t]

The menu, please.

Menuen, tak.
[me'nyən, tak]

Are you ready to order?

Er du klar til at bestille?
[æɐ̯ du klɑ' te ʌ be'stel'ə?]

What will you have?

Hvad vil du have?
['vað ve du hæ'?]

I'll have ...

Jeg vil gerne have ...
[jɑj ve 'gæɐ̯nə hæ' ...]

I'm a vegetarian.

Jeg er vegetar.
['jɑj 'æɐ̯ vegə'tɑ']

meat

kød
['køð]

fish

fisk
['fesk]

vegetables

grøntsager
['gʁɶnt,sæ'jʌ]

Do you have vegetarian dishes?

Har du vegetarretter?
['hɑ' du vegə'tɑ'ʁatə?]

I don't eat pork.

Jeg spiser ikke svinekød.
[jɑ 'spi:sɐ 'ekə 'svi:nə'køð]

He /she/ doesn't eat meat.

Han /hun/ spiser ikke kød.
[han /hun/ 'spi:sɐ 'ekə 'køð]

I am allergic to ...

Jeg er allergisk over for ...
['jɑj 'æɐ̯ a'læɐ̯'gisk 'ɒw'ʌ fə ...]

Would you please bring me ...	**Er du sød at give mig ...** [æɐ̯ du 'søð' ʌ 'gi' maj ...]
salt | pepper | sugar	**salt | peber | sukker** ['sal'̩t | 'pewʌ | 'sɔkʌ]
coffee | tea | dessert	**kaffe | te | dessert** ['kafə | te' | de'sɛɐ̯'t]
water | sparkling | plain	**vand | med brus | uden brus** ['van' | mɛ 'bʁu's | 'uðən 'bʁu's]
a spoon | fork | knife	**en ske | gaffel | kniv** [en ske' | 'gafəl | 'kniw']
a plate | napkin	**en tallerken | serviet** [en ta'læɐ̯kən | sæɐ̯vi'ɛt]

Enjoy your meal!	**Nyd dit måltid!** [nyð dit 'mʌlˌtið']
One more, please.	**En til, tak.** [en te, tak]
It was very delicious.	**Det var meget lækkert.** [de va 'maɑð 'lɛkʌt]

check | change | tip	**regningen | byttepenge | drikkepenge** ['ʁajneŋən | 'bytəˌpɛŋə | 'dʁɛkəˌpɛŋə]
Check, please. (Could I have the check, please?)	**Regningen, tak.** ['ʁajneŋən, tak]
Can I pay by credit card?	**Kan jeg betale med kreditkort?** ['kan' ja be'tæ'lə mɛ kʁe'dit kɔ:t?]
I'm sorry, there's a mistake here.	**Undskyld, men der er en fejl her.** ['ɔnˌskyl', mɛn 'dɛ'ɐ̯ 'æɐ̯ en 'faj'l 'hɛ'ɐ̯]

Shopping

Can I help you?	**Kan jeg hjælpe?** ['kan' jɑ 'jɛlpə?]
Do you have ...?	**Har du ...?** ['hɑ' du ...?]
I'm looking for ...	**Jeg leder efter ...** [jɑ 'leːðə 'ɛftʌ ...]
I need ...	**Jeg har brug for ...** [jɑ hɑ' 'bʁuˀ fə ...]

I'm just looking.	**Jeg kigger bare.** [jɑ 'kigʌ 'bɑːɑ]
We're just looking.	**Vi kiggede bare.** ['vi 'kigəðə 'bɑːɑ]
I'll come back later.	**Jeg kommer tilbage senere.** [jɑ 'kʌmʌ te'bæːjə 'seˀnʌʌ]
We'll come back later.	**Vi kommer tilbage senere.** ['vi 'kʌmʌ te'bæːjə 'seˀnʌʌ]
discounts | sale	**rabatter | udsalg** [ʁɑ'batʌ | 'uðˌsalˀ]

Would you please show me ...	**Vil du være sød at vise mig ...** ['ve du 'vɛ̞' søðˀ ʌ 'viːsə mɑj ...]
Would you please give me ...	**Vil du give mig ...** ['ve du giˀ mɑj ...]
Can I try it on?	**Kan jeg prøve det på?** ['kanˀ jɑ 'pʁœːwə de pɔ'?]
Excuse me, where's the fitting room?	**Undskyld, hvor er prøverummet?** ['ɔnˌskylˀ, vɒˀ 'æ̞ 'pʁœːwə 'ʁɔməð?]
Which color would you like?	**Hvilken farve vil du have?** ['velkən 'fɑːvə ve du hæˀ?]
size | length	**størrelse | længde** ['stœ̞ʌlsə | 'lɛŋˀdə]
How does it fit?	**Hvordan passer det?** [vɒ'dan 'pasʌ de?]

How much is it?	**Hvor meget bliver det?** [vɒˀ 'mɑɑð 'bliˀ de?]
That's too expensive.	**Det er for dyrt.** [de 'æ̞ fə 'dyɐ̯ˀt]
I'll take it.	**Det tager jeg.** [de 'tæˀ ̞ jɑj]
Excuse me, where do I pay?	**Undskyld, hvor kan jeg betale?** ['ɔnˌskylˀ, vɒˀ kanˀ jɑ be'tæˀlə?]

Will you pay in cash or credit card?

Vil du betale kontant eller med kreditkort?
['ve du be'tæ'le kɔn'tan't mɛ kʁɛ'dit kɔ:t?]

In cash | with credit card

Kontant | med kreditkort
[kɔn'tan't | mɛ kʁɛ'dit kɔ:t]

Do you want the receipt?

Vil du have kvitteringen?
['ve du hæ' kvi'te'ʁeŋən?]

Yes, please.

Ja, tak.
['jæ, tɑk]

No, it's OK.

Nej, det er OK.
[nɑj', de 'æɡ ɔw'kɛj]

Thank you. Have a nice day!

Tak. Hav en dejlig dag!
[tɑk. 'hɑ' en 'dɑjli 'dæ']

In town

Excuse me, please.	**Undskyld mig.** ['ɔnˌskyl' mɑj]
I'm looking for ...	**Jeg leder efter ...** [jɑ 'leːðə 'ɛftʌ ...]
the subway	**metroen** ['meːtʁoən]
my hotel	**mit hotel** [mit ho'tɛl']
the movie theater	**biografen** [bio'gʁɑ'fən]
a taxi stand	**en taxiholdeplads** [en 'tɑksi 'hʌləˌplas]
an ATM	**en udbetalingsautomat** [en uð'be'tæ'leŋs ɑwto'mæ't]
a foreign exchange office	**et vekselkontor** [et 'vɛksəl kɔn'to'ɐ̯]
an internet café	**en internetcafé** [en 'entʌˌnɛt ka'fe']
... street	**... gade** [... 'gæːðə]
this place	**dette sted** ['dɛtə 'stɛð]
Do you know where ... is?	**Ved du, hvor ... er?** [ve du, vɒ' ... 'æɐ̯?]
Which street is this?	**Hvilken gade er dette?** ['velkən 'gæːðə 'æɐ̯ 'dɛtə?]
Show me where we are right now.	**Vis mig, hvor vi er lige nu.** ['vi's mɑj, vɒ' vi 'æɐ̯ 'liːə nu]
Can I get there on foot?	**Kan jeg komme derhen til fods?** ['kan' jɑ 'kʌmə 'dɛ'ɐ̯'hɛn te 'fo'ðs?]
Do you have a map of the city?	**Har du et kort over byen?** ['hɑ' du et 'kɒːt 'ɒwˀʌ 'byən?]
How much is a ticket to get in?	**Hvor meget koster en billet** **for at komme ind?** [vɒ' 'mɑɑð 'kʌstɐ en bi'lɛt fə ʌ 'kʌmə 'en'?]
Can I take pictures here?	**Må jeg tage billeder her?** [mɔ' jɑ tæ' 'beləðʌ 'hɛ'ɐ̯?]
Are you open?	**Har du åbent?** ['hɑ' du 'ɔːbənt?]

When do you open?

Hvornår åbner du?
[vɒˈnɒˀ ˈɔːbnʌ duˀ]

When do you close?

Hvornår lukker du?
[vɒˈnɒˀ ˈlɔkɐ duˀ]

Money

money	**penge** ['pɛŋə]
cash	**kontanter** [kɔn'tanˀtʌ]
paper money	**sedler** ['sɛðˀlʌ]
loose change	**småmønter** [ˌsmʌ'mønˀtʌ]
check | change | tip	**regningen | byttepenge | drikkepenge** ['ʁɑjneŋən | 'bytəˌpɛŋə | 'dʁɛkəˌpɛŋə]

credit card	**kreditkort** [kʁɛ'dit kɔːt]
wallet	**tegnebog** ['tɑjnəbɔˀw]
to buy	**at købe** [ʌ 'køːbə]
to pay	**at betale** [ʌ be'tæˀlə]
fine	**bøde** ['bøːðə]
free	**gratis** ['gʁɑːtis]

Where can I buy ...?	**Hvor kan jeg købe ...?** [vɒˀ kan ja 'køːbə ...?]
Is the bank open now?	**Har banken åbent nu?** ['hɑˀ 'baŋkən 'ɔːbənt nu?]
When does it open?	**Hvornår åbner den?** [vɒ'nɒˀ 'ɔːbnʌ dɛnˀ?]
When does it close?	**Hvornår lukker den?** [vɒ'nɒˀ 'lɔkɐ dɛnˀ?]

How much?	**Hvor meget?** [vɒˀ 'mɑɑðˀ?]
How much is this?	**Hvor meget bliver det?** [vɒˀ 'mɑɑð 'bliɐˀ deˀ?]
That's too expensive.	**Det er for dyrt.** [de 'æɐ̯ fə 'dyɐ̯ˀt]

Excuse me, where do I pay?	**Undskyld, hvor kan jeg betale?** ['ɔnˌskylˀ, vɒˀ kanˀ ja be'tæˀlə?]
Check, please.	**Regningen, tak.** ['ʁɑjneŋən, tak]

Can I pay by credit card?

Kan jeg betale med kreditkort?
['kan' ja be'tæ'lə mɛ kʁɛ'dit kɒ:t?]

Is there an ATM here?

**Er der en
udbetalingsautomat her?**
[æɐ̯ 'dɛ'ɐ̯ en
uð'be'tæ'leŋs ɑwto'mæ't 'hɛ'ɐ̯?]

I'm looking for an ATM.

**Jeg leder efter
en udbetalingsautomat.**
[ja 'le:ðə 'ɛftʌ
en uð'be'tæ'leŋs ɑwto'mæ't]

I'm looking for a foreign exchange office.

Jeg leder efter et vekselkontor.
[ja 'le:ðə 'ɛftʌ et 'vɛksəl kɔn'to'ɐ̯]

I'd like to change ...

Jeg vil gerne veksle ...
[jaj ve 'gæɐ̯nə 'vɛkslə ...]

What is the exchange rate?

Hvad er vekselkursen?
['vað 'æɐ̯ 'vɛksəl 'kuɐ̯'sən]

Do you need my passport?

Har du brug for mit pas?
['ha' du 'bʁu' fə mit 'pas?]

Time

What time is it?	**Hvad er klokken?** ['vað 'æɐ̯ 'klʌkən?]
When?	**Hvornår?** [vɒ'nɒˀ?]
At what time?	**På hvilket tidspunkt?** [pɔ 'velkəð 'tiðspɔŋˀtˀ?]
now | later | after ...	**nu | senere | efter ...** ['nu | 'seˀnʌʌ | 'ɛftʌ ...]
one o'clock	**klokken et** ['klʌkən et]
one fifteen	**kvart over et** ['kvɑːt 'ɒwˀʌ et]
one thirty	**halv to** ['halˀ 'toˀ]
one forty-five	**kvart i to** ['kvɑːt i 'toˀ]

one | two | three	**et | to | tre** [ed | toˀ | tʁɛˀ]
four | five | six	**fire | fem | seks** ['fiˀʌ | fɛmˀ | 'sɛks]
seven | eight | nine	**syv | otte | ni** ['sywˀ | 'ɔːtə | niˀ]
ten | eleven | twelve	**ti | elleve | tolv** ['tiˀ | 'ɛlvə | tʌlˀ]

in ...	**om ...** [ʌm ...]
five minutes	**fem minutter** [fɛmˀ me'nutʌ]
ten minutes	**ti minutter** ['tiˀ me'nutʌ]
fifteen minutes	**femten minutter** ['fɛmtən me'nutʌ]
twenty minutes	**tyve minutter** ['tyːvə me'nutʌ]
half an hour	**en halv time** [en 'halˀ 'tiːmə]
an hour	**en time** [en 'tiːmə]
in the morning	**om morgenen** [ʌm 'mɒːɒnən]
early in the morning	**tidligt om morgenen** ['tiðlit ʌm 'mɒːɒnən]

this morning	**her til morgen** ['hɛ'ɐ̯ te 'mɒːɒn]
tomorrow morning	**i morgen tidlig** [i 'mɒːɒn 'tiðli]

in the middle of the day	**midt på dagen** ['met pɔ 'dæ'ən]
in the afternoon	**om eftermiddagen** [ʌm 'ɛftʌme̩dæ'ən]
in the evening	**om aftenen** [ʌm 'ɑftənən]
tonight	**i aften** [i 'ɑftən]

at night	**om natten** [ʌm 'nɛtn]
yesterday	**i går** [i 'gɒ']
today	**i dag** [i 'dæ']
tomorrow	**i morgen** [i 'mɒːɒn]
the day after tomorrow	**i overmorgen** [i 'ɒwʌmɒːɒn]

What day is it today?	**Hvilken dag er det i dag?** ['velkən 'dæ' 'æɐ̯ de i 'dæ'?]
It's ...	**Det er ...** [de 'æɐ̯ ...]
Monday	**Mandag** ['man'da]
Tuesday	**tirsdag** ['tiɐ̯'sda]
Wednesday	**onsdag** ['ɔn'sda]

Thursday	**torsdag** ['tɒ'sda]
Friday	**Fredag** ['fʁɛ'da]
Saturday	**Lørdag** ['lœɐ̯da]
Sunday	**søndag** ['sœn'da]

Greetings. Introductions

Hello.
Hej.
['hɑj]

Pleased to meet you.
Glad for at møde dig.
['glað fə ʌ 'mø:ðə 'dɑj]

Me too.
Det samme her.
[de 'samə 'hɛˀɐ̯]

I'd like you to meet …
Jeg vil gerne have at du møder …
[jɑj ve 'gæɐ̯nə hæˀ ʌ du 'mø:ðə …]

Nice to meet you.
Rart at møde dig.
['ʁɑˀt ʌ 'mø:ðə dɑj]

How are you?
Hvordan har du det?
[vɒ'dan hɑˀ du de?]

My name is …
Mit navn er …
[mit 'nɑwˀn 'æɐ̯ …]

His name is …
Hans navn er …
[hans 'nɑwˀn 'æɐ̯ …]

Her name is …
Hendes navn er …
['henəs 'nɑwˀn 'æɐ̯ …]

What's your name?
Hvad hedder du?
['vað 'heðʌ du?]

What's his name?
Hvad hedder han?
['vað 'heðʌ han?]

What's her name?
Hvad hedder hun?
['vað 'heðʌ hun?]

What's your last name?
Hvad er dit efternavn?
['vað 'æɐ̯ did 'ɛftʌˌnɑwˀn?]

You can call me …
Du kan ringe til mig …
[du kan 'ʁɐŋə te mɑj …]

Where are you from?
Hvor er du fra?
[vɒˀ 'æɐ̯ du fʁɑˀ]

I'm from …
Jeg er fra …
['jɑj 'æɐ̯ fʁɑˀ …]

What do you do for a living?
Hvad arbejder du med?
['vað 'ɑːˌbɑjˀdʌ du mɛ?]

Who is this?
Hvem er det?
[vɛm 'æɐ̯ de?]

Who is he?
Hvem er han?
[vɛm 'æɐ̯ han?]

Who is she?
Hvem er hun?
[vɛm 'æɐ̯ hun?]

Who are they?	**Hvem er de?** [vɛm 'æɐ̯ di?]
This is ...	**Dette er ...** ['dɛtə 'æɐ̯ ...]
my friend (masc.)	**min ven** [min 'vɛn]
my friend (fem.)	**min veninde** [min vɛn'enə]
my husband	**min mand** [min 'manˀ]
my wife	**min kone** [min 'koːnə]

my father	**min far** [min 'fɑː]
my mother	**min mor** [min 'moɐ̯]
my brother	**min bror** [min 'bʁoɐ̯]
my sister	**min søster** [min 'søstʌ]
my son	**min søn** [min 'sœn]
my daughter	**min datter** [min 'datʌ]

This is our son.	**Dette er vores søn.** ['dɛtə 'æɐ̯ 'vɒs 'sœn]
This is our daughter.	**Dette er vores datter.** ['dɛtə 'æɐ̯ 'vɒs 'datʌ]
These are my children.	**Dette er mine børn.** ['dɛtə 'æɐ̯ 'miːnə 'bœɐ̯ˀn]
These are our children.	**Dette er vores børn.** ['dɛtə 'æɐ̯ 'vɒs 'bœɐ̯ˀn]

Farewells

Good bye!	**Farvel!** [fɑ'vɛl]
Bye! (inform.)	**Hej hej!** ['hɑj 'hɑj]
See you tomorrow.	**Ses i morgen.** ['seʔs i 'mɒːɒn]
See you soon.	**Vi ses snart.** ['vi 'seʔs 'snɑʔt]
See you at seven.	**Vi ses klokken syv.** ['vi 'seʔs 'klʌkən 'sywʔ]
Have fun!	**Have det sjovt!** ['haʔ de 'ɕɒwd]
Talk to you later.	**Vi snakkes ved senere.** ['vi 'snɑkəs ve 'seʔnʌʌ]
Have a nice weekend.	**Ha' en dejlig weekend.** [ha en 'dɑjli 'wiːˌkɛnd]
Good night.	**Godnat.** [go'nad]
It's time for me to go.	**Det er på tide at jeg smutter.** [de 'æɡ pɒ 'tiːðə ʌ jɑ 'smutə]
I have to go.	**Jeg bliver nødt til at gå.** [jɑ 'bliɡʔ nøʔt te ʌ 'ɡɔʔ]
I will be right back.	**Jeg kommer straks tilbage.** [jɑ 'kʌmʌ 'stʁɑks te'bæːjə]
It's late.	**Det er sent.** [de 'æɡ 'seʔnt]
I have to get up early.	**Jeg er nødt til at stå tidligt op.** ['jɑj 'æɡ nøʔt te ʌ 'stɔʔ 'tiðlit 'ʌp]
I'm leaving tomorrow.	**Jeg rejser i morgen.** [jɑ 'ʁɑjsə i 'mɒːɒn]
We're leaving tomorrow.	**Vi rejser i morgen.** ['vi 'ʁɑjsə i 'mɒːɒn]
Have a nice trip!	**Hav en dejlig tur!** ['haʔ en 'dɑjli 'tuɡʔ]
It was nice meeting you.	**Det var rart at møde dig.** [de vɑ 'ʁɑʔt ʌ 'møːðə 'dɑj]
It was nice talking to you.	**Det var rart at tale med dig.** [de vɑ 'ʁɑʔt ʌ 'tæːlə mɛ 'dɑj]
Thanks for everything.	**Tak for alt.** [tɑk fə 'alʔt]

I had a very good time.

Jeg nød tiden sammen.
[ja nø:ð 'tiðən 'sam'ən]

We had a very good time.

Vi nød virkeligt tiden sammen.
['vi nø:ð 'viɐ̯kəlit 'tiðən 'sam'ən]

It was really great.

Det var virkeligt godt.
[de va 'viɐ̯kəlit 'gʌt]

I'm going to miss you.

Jeg kommer til at savne dig.
[ja 'kʌmʌ te ʌ 'sawne 'daj]

We're going to miss you.

Vi kommer til at savne dig.
['vi 'kʌmʌ te ʌ 'sawne 'daj]

Good luck!

Held og lykke!
['hɛl' ʌ 'løkə]

Say hi to ...

Sig hej til ...
['saj 'haj te ...]

Foreign language

I don't understand.	**Jeg forstår det ikke.** [ja fə'stɐ de 'ekə]
Write it down, please.	**Skriv det ned, tak.** ['skʁiw' de neð', tɑk]
Do you speak ...?	**Taler du ...?** ['tæːlʌ du ...?]

I speak a little bit of ...	**Jeg taler en lille smule ...** [ja 'tæːlʌ en 'lilə 'smuːlə ...]
English	**engelsk** ['ɛŋˀəlsk]
Turkish	**tyrkisk** ['tyɐkisk]
Arabic	**arabisk** [ɑ'ʁɑˀbisk]
French	**fransk** ['fʁɑnˀsk]

German	**tysk** ['tysk]
Italian	**italiensk** [ital'jɛˀnsk]
Spanish	**spansk** ['spanˀsk]
Portuguese	**portugisisk** [pɒtu'giˀsisk]
Chinese	**kinesisk** [ki'neˀsisk]
Japanese	**japansk** [ja'pæˀnsk]

Can you repeat that, please.	**Kan du gentage det, tak.** ['kan du 'gɛn̩ˌtæˀ de, tɑk]
I understand.	**Jeg forstår.** [ja fə'stɐ]
I don't understand.	**Jeg forstår det ikke.** [ja fə'stɐ de 'ekə]
Please speak more slowly.	**Tal langsommere.** ['tal 'laŋˌsʌmˀəʌ]

Is that correct? (Am I saying it right?)	**Er det rigtigt?** [æɐ de 'ʁɛgtit?]
What is this? (What does this mean?)	**Hvad er dette?** ['vað 'æɐ 'dɛtə?]

Apologies

Excuse me, please.

Undskyld mig.
[ˈɔnˌskylˀ majˀ]

I'm sorry.

Det er jeg ked af.
[de ˈæɐ̯ ja ˈkeðˀ æˀ]

I'm really sorry.

Jeg er virkelig ked af det.
[ˈjaj ˈæɐ̯ ˈviɐ̯kəli ˈkeðˀ æˀ de]

Sorry, it's my fault.

Beklager, det er min skyld.
[beˈklæˀjə, de ˈæɐ̯ min ˈskylˀ]

My mistake.

Min fejl.
[min ˈfajˀl]

May I ...?

Må jeg ...?
[mɔˀ ja ...?]

Do you mind if I ...?

Har du noget imod, hvis jeg ...?
[ˈhaˀ du ˈnoːəð iˈmoðˀ, ˈves jaj ...?]

It's OK.

Det er OK.
[de ˈæɐ̯ ɔwˈkɛj]

It's all right.

Det er OK.
[de ˈæɐ̯ ɔwˈkɛj]

Don't worry about it.

Tag dig ikke af det.
[ˈtæˀ ˈdaj ˈekə æˀ de]

Agreement

Yes. | **Ja.**
['jæ]

Yes, sure. | **Ja, helt sikkert.**
['jæ, 'heˀlt 'sekʌt]

OK (Good!) | **Godt!**
['gʌt]

Very well. | **Meget godt.**
['maɑð 'gʌt]

Certainly! | **Bestemt!**
[be'stɛmˀt]

I agree. | **Jeg er enig.**
['jɑj 'æɐ̯ 'eːni]

That's correct. | **Det er korrekt.**
[de 'æɐ̯ ko'ʁakt]

That's right. | **Det er rigtigt.**
[de 'æɐ̯ 'ʁɛgtit]

You're right. | **Du har ret.**
[du hɑˀ 'ʁat]

I don't mind. | **Jeg har ikke noget imod det.**
[jɑ hɑˀ 'eke 'noːɐð i'moðˀ de]

Absolutely right. | **Helt korrekt.**
['heˀlt ko'ʁakt]

It's possible. | **Det er muligt.**
[de 'æɐ̯ 'muːlit]

That's a good idea. | **Det er en god idé.**
[de 'æɐ̯ en 'goðˀ i'deˀ]

I can't say no. | **Jeg kan ikke sige nej.**
[jɑ kan 'eke 'siː 'nɑjˀ]

I'd be happy to. | **Jeg ville være glad for.**
[jɑj 'vile 'vɛɐ̯ˀ 'glað fə]

With pleasure. | **Med glæde.**
[mɛ 'glɛːðə]

Refusal. Expressing doubt

No.

Nej.
[nɑjˀ]

Certainly not.

Bestemt ikke.
[be'stɛmˀt 'ekə]

I don't agree.

Jeg er ikke enig.
['jɑj 'æɐ̯ 'ekə 'eːni]

I don't think so.

Jeg tror det ikke.
[jɑ 'tʁoˀɐ̯ de 'ekə]

It's not true.

Det er ikke sandt.
[de 'æɐ̯ 'ekə 'sant]

You are wrong.

Du tager fejl.
[du 'tæˀɐ̯ 'fɑjˀl]

I think you are wrong.

Jeg tror, du tager fejl.
[jɑ 'tʁoˀɐ̯, du 'tæˀɐ̯ 'fɑjˀl]

I'm not sure.

Jeg er ikke sikker.
['jɑj 'æɐ̯ 'ekə 'sekʌ]

It's impossible.

Det er umuligt.
[de 'æɐ̯ u'muˀlit]

Nothing of the kind (sort)!

Overhovedet ikke!
[ɒwʌ'hoːədəð 'ekə]

The exact opposite.

Det stik modsatte.
[de 'stek 'moðˌsatə]

I'm against it.

Jeg er imod det.
['jɑj 'æɐ̯ i'moðˀ de]

I don't care.

Jeg er ligeglad.
['jɑj 'æɐ̯ 'liːəˌglað]

I have no idea.

Jeg aner det ikke.
['jɑj 'æːnə de 'ekə]

I doubt it.

Jeg tvivler på det.
[jɑ 'tviwlə pɔˀ de]

Sorry, I can't.

Undskyld, jeg kan ikke.
['ɔnˌskylˀ, jɑ kanˀ 'ekə]

Sorry, I don't want to.

Undskyld, jeg ønsker ikke at.
['ɔnˌskylˀ, jɑ 'ønskɐ 'ekə ʌ]

Thank you, but I don't need this.

Tak, men jeg har ikke brug for dette.
[tak, mɛn jɑ 'hɑˀ 'ekə 'bʁuˀ fə 'dɛtə]

It's getting late.

Det bliver sent.
[de 'bliɐ̯ˀ 'seˀnt]

I have to get up early.

Jeg er nødt til at stå tidligt op.
['jɑj 'æɐ̯ nø'̍t te ʌ 'stɔˀ 'tiðlit ʌp]

I don't feel well.

Jeg føler mig dårlig.
[jɑ 'fø:lɐ mɑj 'dɒ:li]

Expressing gratitude

Thank you.	**Tak.** [tɑk]
Thank you very much.	**Mange tak.** ['mɑŋə 'tɑk]
I really appreciate it.	**Jeg sætter virkeligt pris på det.** [ja sɛtʌ 'viɐ̯kəlit 'pʁis pɔ' de]
I'm really grateful to you.	**Jeg er dig virkeligt taknemmelig.** ['jaj 'æɐ̯ dɑ 'viɐ̯kəlit tɑk'nɛm'əli]
We are really grateful to you.	**Vi er dig virkeligt taknemmelige.** ['vi 'æɐ̯ dɑ 'viɐ̯kəlit tɑk'nɛm'əliə]
Thank you for your time.	**Tak for din tid.** [tɑk fə din 'tið']
Thanks for everything.	**Tak for alt.** [tɑk fə 'al'̯t]
Thank you for …	**Tak for …** [tɑk fə …]
your help	**din hjælp** [din 'jɛl'p]
a nice time	**en dejlig tid** [en 'dɑjli 'tið']
a wonderful meal	**et vidunderligt måltid** [ed við'ɔn'ʌlit 'mʌlˌtið']
a pleasant evening	**en hyggelig aften** [en 'hygəli 'aftən]
a wonderful day	**en vidunderlig dag** [en við'ɔn'ʌli 'dæ']
an amazing journey	**en fantastisk rejse** [en fan'tastisk 'ʁɑjsə]
Don't mention it.	**Glem det.** ['glɛm de]
You are welcome.	**Du er velkommen.** [du 'æɐ̯ 'vɛlˌkʌm'ən]
Any time.	**Når som helst.** ['nɒ' sʌm 'hɛl'st]
My pleasure.	**Intet problem.** ['entəð pʁo'ble'm]
Forget it.	**Glem det.** ['glɛm de]
Don't worry about it.	**Tag dig ikke af det.** ['tæ' 'dɑj 'ekə æ' de]

Congratulations. Best wishes

Congratulations!

Til lykke!
[te 'løkə]

Happy birthday!

Tillykke med fødselsdagen!
[tə'løkə mɛ 'føsəlsˌdæˀən]

Merry Christmas!

Glædelig jul!
['glɛːðəli 'juˀl]

Happy New Year!

Godt Nytår!
['gʌt 'nytˌɒˀ]

Happy Easter!

God påske!
['goðˀ 'pɒːskə]

Happy Hanukkah!

Glædelig Hanukkah!
['glɛːðəli 'hanuka]

I'd like to propose a toast.

Jeg vil gerne udbringe en skål.
[jɑj ve 'gæɐ̯nə 'uðˌbʁɛŋˀə en 'skɔˀl]

Cheers!

Skål!
['skɔˀl]

Let's drink to ...!

Lad os skåle for ...!
[laðˀ ʌs 'skɔːlə fə ...!]

To our success!

Til vores succes!
[te 'vɒɒs syk'se]

To your success!

Til din succes!
[te din syk'se]

Good luck!

Held og lykke!
['hɛlˀ ʌ 'løkə]

Have a nice day!

Hav en dejlig dag!
['haˀ en 'dɑjli 'dæˀ]

Have a good holiday!

Hav en god ferie!
['haˀ en 'goðˀ 'feɐ̯ˀiə]

Have a safe journey!

Har en sikker rejse!
['haˀ en 'sekʌ 'ʁɑjsə!]

I hope you get better soon!

Jeg håber du får det bedre snart!
[jɑ 'hɔːbʌ du fɒˀ de 'bɛðʁʌ 'snɑˀt]

Socializing

Why are you sad?	**Hvorfor er du ked af det?** ['vɔfʌ 'æɐ̯ du 'keð' æ' de?]
Smile! Cheer up!	**Smil! Op med humøret!** ['smi'l! ʌb mɛ hu'mø'ɐ̯əð]
Are you free tonight?	**Er du fri i aften?** [æɐ̯ du 'fʁi' i 'ɑftən?]
May I offer you a drink?	**Må jeg tilbyde dig en drink?** [mɔ' jɑ 'tel‚by'ðə 'dɑj en 'driŋk?]
Would you like to dance?	**Kunne du tænke dig at danse?** ['kunə du 'tɛŋkə dɑj ʌ 'dansə?]
Let's go to the movies.	**Lad os gå i biografen.** [lað ʌs 'gɔ' i bio'gʁɑ'fən]
May I invite you to ...?	**Må jeg invitere dig til ...?** [mɔ' jɑ envi'te'ʌ dɑ te ...?]
a restaurant	**en restaurant** [en ʁɛsto'ʁɑŋ]
the movies	**biografen** [bio'gʁɑ'fən]
the theater	**teatret** [te'æ'tɐ̯əð]
go for a walk	**at gå en tur** [ʌ 'gɔ' en 'tuɐ̯']
At what time?	**På hvilket tidspunkt?** [pɔ 'velkəð 'tiðspɔŋ't?]
tonight	**i aften** [i 'ɑftən]
at six	**klokken seks** ['klʌkən 'sɛks]
at seven	**klokken syv** ['klʌkən 'syw']
at eight	**klokken otte** ['klʌkən 'ɔ:tə]
at nine	**klokken ni** ['klʌkən 'ni']
Do you like it here?	**Kan du lide det her?** ['kan du 'li:ðə de 'hɛ'ɐ̯?]
Are you here with someone?	**Er du her med nogen?** [æɐ̯ du 'hɛ'ɐ̯ mɛ 'noən?]
I'm with my friend.	**Jeg er sammen med min ven.** ['jɑj 'æɐ̯ 'sɑm'ən mɛ min 'vɛn]

I'm with my friends.

Jeg er sammen med mine venner.
['jɑj 'æɡ 'samˀən mɛ'miːnə 'vɛnʌ]

No, I'm alone.

Nej, jeg er alene.
[nɑjˀ, jɑ 'æɡ a'leːnə]

Do you have a boyfriend?

Har du en kæreste?
['hɑˀ du en 'kæɡʌstə?]

I have a boyfriend.

Jeg har en kæreste.
[jɑ hɑˀ en 'kæɡʌstə]

Do you have a girlfriend?

Har du en kæreste?
['hɑˀ du en 'kæɡʌstə?]

I have a girlfriend.

Jeg har en kæreste.
[jɑ hɑˀ en 'kæɡʌstə]

Can I see you again?

Kan jeg se dig igen?
['kanˀ jɑ seˀ dɑj i'ɡɛn?]

Can I call you?

Kan jeg ringe til dig?
['kanˀ jɑ 'ʁɛŋə te dɑj?]

Call me. (Give me a call.)

Ring til mig.
['ʁɛŋə te mɑj]

What's your number?

Hvad er dit nummer?
['vað 'æɡ dit 'nɔmˀʌ?]

I miss you.

Jeg savner dig.
[jɑ 'sɑwnɡ dɑj]

You have a beautiful name.

Du har et smukt navn.
[du hɑˀ et 'smɔkt 'nɑwˀn]

I love you.

Jeg elsker dig.
['jɑj 'ɛlskʌ dɑj]

Will you marry me?

Vil du gifte dig med mig?
['ve du 'ɡiftə 'dɑj mɛ mɑj?]

You're kidding!

Du spøger!
[du 'spøːjə]

I'm just kidding.

Jeg spøger.
[jɑ 'spøːjə]

Are you serious?

Mener du det alvorligt?
['meːnʌ du de al'vɒˀlit?]

I'm serious.

Jeg mener det alvorligt.
[jɑ 'meːnʌ de al'vɒˀlit]

Really?!

Virkeligt?!
['viɡkəlit?!]

It's unbelievable!

Det er utroligt!
[de 'æɡ u'tʁoˀlit]

I don't believe you.

Jeg tror dig ikke.
[jɑ 'tʁoˀɡ 'dɑj 'ekə]

I can't.

Jeg kan ikke.
[jɑ kan 'ekə]

I don't know.

Jeg ved det ikke.
[jɑj ve de 'ekə]

I don't understand you.

Jeg forstår dig ikke.
[ja fə'stɐ̯ daj 'ekə]

Please go away.

Gå din vej.
['gɔ' din 'vaj']

Leave me alone!

Lad mig være!
[lað maj 'vɛɐ̯']

I can't stand him.

Jeg kan ikke fordrage ham.
[ja kan 'ekə fə'dʀɑ'wə ham]

You are disgusting!

Du er modbydelig!
[du 'æɐ̯ moð'byð'əli]

I'll call the police!

Jeg ringer til politiet!
[ja 'ʀɛŋʌ te poli'ti'əð]

Sharing impressions. Emotions

I like it.	**Jeg kan lide det.** [ja kan 'li:ðə de]
Very nice.	**Meget fint.** ['maað 'fi'nt]
That's great!	**Det er godt!** [de 'æɐ̯ 'gʌt]
It's not bad.	**Det er ikke dårligt.** [de 'æɐ̯ 'ekə 'dɔ:lit]

I don't like it.	**Jeg kan ikke lide det.** [ja kan 'ekə 'li:ðə de]
It's not good.	**Det er ikke godt.** [de 'æɐ̯ 'ekə 'gʌt]
It's bad.	**Det er dårligt.** [de 'æɐ̯ 'dɔ:lit]
It's very bad.	**Det er meget dårligt.** [de 'æɐ̯ 'maað 'dɔ:lit]
It's disgusting.	**Det er ulækkert.** [de 'æɐ̯ 'uˌlɛkʌt]

I'm happy.	**Jeg er glad.** ['jaj 'æɐ̯ 'glað]
I'm content.	**Jeg er tilfreds.** ['jaj 'æɐ̯ te'fʁɛs]
I'm in love.	**Jeg er forelsket.** ['jaj 'æɐ̯ fə'ɛl'skəð]
I'm calm.	**Jeg er rolig.** ['jaj 'æɐ̯ 'ʁo:li]
I'm bored.	**Jeg keder mig.** [ja 'ke:ðʌ maj]

I'm tired.	**Jeg er træt.** ['jaj 'æɐ̯ 'tʁat]
I'm sad.	**Jeg er ked af det.** ['jaj 'æɐ̯ 'keð' æ' de]
I'm frightened.	**Jeg er bange.** ['jaj 'æɐ̯ 'baŋə]

I'm angry.	**Jeg er vred.** ['jaj 'æɐ̯ 'vʁɛð']
I'm worried.	**Jeg er bekymret.** ['jaj 'æɐ̯ be'køm'ʁʌð]
I'm nervous.	**Jeg er nervøs.** ['jaj 'æɐ̯ næɐ̯'vø's]

I'm jealous. (envious)

Jeg er misundelig.
['jɑj 'æɐ̯ mis'ɔn'əli]

I'm surprised.

Jeg er overrasket.
['jɑj 'æɐ̯ 'ɒwʌˌʁaskəð]

I'm perplexed.

Jeg er forvirret.
['jɑj 'æɐ̯ fʌ'viɐ̯'ʌð]

Problems. Accidents

I've got a problem.	**Jeg har fået et problem.** [ja haˀ fʊˀ et pʁoˈbleˀm]
We've got a problem,	**Vi har fået et problem.** [ˈvi haˀ ˈfʊˀ et pʁoˈbleˀm]
I'm lost.	**Jeg forstår ikke.** [ja fəˈstǫ ˈekə]
I missed the last bus (train).	**Jeg kom for sent til den sidste bus (tog).** [ja ˈkʌmˀ fə ˈseˀnt te dən ˈsistə bus (ˈtɔˀw)]
I don't have any money left.	**Jeg har ikke nogen penge tilbage.** [ja haˀ ˈekə ˈnoən ˈpɛŋə teˈbæːjə]

I've lost my ...	**Jeg har mistet min ...** [ja haˀ ˈmestəð min ...]
Someone stole my ...	**Nogen stjal mit ...** [ˈnoən ˈstjæˀl mit ...]
passport	**pas** [ˈpas]
wallet	**tegnebog** [ˈtɑjnəbɔˀw]
papers	**papirer** [paˈpiːɐ̯ˀ]
ticket	**billet** [biˈlɛt]
money	**penge** [ˈpɛŋə]
handbag	**håndtaske** [ˈhʌnˈtaskə]
camera	**kamera** [ˈkæˀmɐʁɑ]
laptop	**laptop** [ˈlapˌtʌp]
tablet computer	**tablet computer** [ˈtablɛt kʌmˈpjuːtʌ]
mobile phone	**mobiltelefon** [moˈbil teləˈfoˀn]

Help me!	**Hjælp mig!** [ˈjɛlˀp mɑj]
What's happened?	**Hvad er der sket?** [ˈvað ˈæɐ̯ ˈdɛˀɐ̯ ˈskeˀð?]
fire	**brand** [ˈbʁanˀ]

shooting	**skyderi** [skyðʌ'ʁiʔ]
murder	**mord** ['moʔɐ̯]
explosion	**eksplosion** [ɛksplo'ɕoʔn]
fight	**kamp** ['kɑmʔp]

Call the police!	**Ring til politiet!** ['ʁɛŋə te poli'tiʔəð]
Please hurry up!	**Vær sød at skynde dig!** ['vɛɐ̯ʔ 'søðʔ ʌ 'skønə 'dɑj]
I'm looking for the police station.	**Jeg leder efter politistationen.** [jɑ 'leːðə 'ɛftʌ poli'ti sta'ɕoʔnən]
I need to make a call.	**Jeg har brug for at foretage et opkald.** [jɑ hɑʔ 'bʁuʔ fə ʌ 'foːɒ̯ˌtæʔ et 'ʌpkalʔ]
May I use your phone?	**Må jeg bruge din telefon?** [mɔʔ jɑ 'bʁuːə din teləˈfoʔn?]

I've been …	**Jeg er blevet …** ['jɑj 'æɐ̯ 'blewəð …]
mugged	**overfaldet** ['ɒwʌˌfalʔəð]
robbed	**røvet** ['ʁœwəð]
raped	**voldtaget** ['vʌlˌtæʔəð]
attacked (beaten up)	**angrebet** ['anˌgʁɛʔbəð]

Are you all right?	**Er du okay?** [æɐ̯ du ɔw'kɛj?]
Did you see who it was?	**Så du, hvem det var?** ['sɔʔ du, vɛm de 'vɑ?]
Would you be able to recognize the person?	**Ville du være i stand til at genkende personen?** ['vilə du 'vɛɐ̯ʔ i 'stan te ʌ 'gɛnˌkɛnʔə pæɐ̯'soʔnən?]
Are you sure?	**Er du sikker?** ['æɐ̯ du 'sekʌ?]

Please calm down.	**Fald til ro.** ['falʔ te 'ʁoʔ]
Take it easy!	**Tag det roligt!** ['tæʔ de 'ʁoːlit]
Don't worry!	**Det går nok!** [de gɔʔ 'nʌk]
Everything will be fine.	**Alt vil være OK.** ['alʔt ve 'vɛɐ̯ʔ ɔw'kɛj]
Everything's all right.	**Alt er okay.** ['alʔt 'æɐ̯ ɔw'kɛj]

Come here, please.

Kom her.
[kʌmˀ 'hɛˀɐ̯]

I have some questions for you.

Jeg har nogle spørgsmål til dig.
[ja haˀ 'noːlə 'sbœɐ̯sˌmɔˀl te 'daj]

Wait a moment, please.

Vent et øjeblik.
['vɛnt et 'ʌjəˌblek]

Do you have any I.D.?

Har du nogen ID?
['haˀ du 'noən 'iˀˈdeˀ?]

Thanks. You can leave now.

Tak. Du kan gå nu.
[tɑk. du kan 'gɔˀ nu]

Hands behind your head!

Hænderne bag hovedet!
['hɛnˀʌnə 'bæˀ 'hoːðəð]

You're under arrest!

Du er anholdt!
[du 'æɐ̯ 'anˌhʌlt]

Health problems

Please help me.	**Vær sød at hjælpe mig.** ['vɛɐ̯' 'søð' ʌ 'jɛlpə maj]
I don't feel well.	**Jeg føler mig dårlig.** [ja 'fø:lɐ maj 'dɒ:li]
My husband doesn't feel well.	**Min mand føler sig dårlig.** [min 'man' 'fø:lɐ saj 'dɒ:li]
My son ...	**Min søn ...** [min 'sœn ...]
My father ...	**Min far ...** [min 'fɑ: ...]
My wife doesn't feel well.	**Min kone føler sig dårlig.** [min 'ko:nə 'fø:lɐ saj 'dɒ:li]
My daughter ...	**Min datter ...** [min 'datʌ ...]
My mother ...	**Min mor ...** [min 'moɐ̯ ...]
I've got a ...	**Jeg har fået ...** [ja hɑ' fɒ' ...]
headache	**hovedpine** ['ho:əð‚pi:nə]
sore throat	**ondt i halsen** ['ɔnt i 'hal'sən]
stomach ache	**mavepine** ['mæ:və 'pi:nə]
toothache	**tandpine** ['tan‚pi:nə]
I feel dizzy.	**Jeg føler mig svimmel.** [ja 'fø:lɐ maj 'svem'əl]
He has a fever.	**Han har feber.** [han hɑ' 'fe'bʌ]
She has a fever.	**Hun har feber.** [hun hɑ' 'fe'bʌ]
I can't breathe.	**Jeg kan ikke få vejret.** [ja kan 'ekə fɒ' 'vaj‚ʁat]
I'm short of breath.	**Jeg er forpustet.** ['jaj 'æɐ̯ fə'pu'stəð]
I am asthmatic.	**Jeg er astmatiker.** ['jaj 'æɐ̯ ast'mæ'tikʌ]
I am diabetic.	**Jeg er diabetiker.** ['jaj 'æɐ̯ dia'be'tikʌ]

I can't sleep.
Jeg kan ikke sove.
[ja kan 'ekə 'sɒwə]

food poisoning
madforgiftning
['maðfʌˌgiftnen]

It hurts here.
Det gør ondt her.
[de 'gœɐ̯ ɔnt 'hɛˀɐ̯]

Help me!
Hjælp mig!
['jɛlˀp mɑj]

I am here!
Jeg er her!
['jɑj 'æɐ̯ 'hɛˀɐ̯]

We are here!
Vi er her!
['vi 'æɐ̯ 'hɛˀɐ̯]

Get me out of here!
Få mig ud herfra!
['fɔˀ mɑj 'uðˀ 'hɛˀɐ̯ˌfʁɑˀ]

I need a doctor.
Jeg har brug for en læge.
[ja hɑˀ 'bʁuˀ fə en 'lɛːjə]

I can't move.
Jeg kan ikke bevæge sig.
[ja kan 'ekə be'vɛˀjə 'sɑj]

I can't move my legs.
Jeg kan ikke bevæge mine ben.
[ja kan 'ekə be'vɛˀjə 'miːnə 'beˀn]

I have a wound.
Jeg har et sår.
[ja hɑˀ et 'sɒˀ]

Is it serious?
Er det alvorligt?
[æɐ̯ de al'vɒˀlit?]

My documents are in my pocket.
Mine papirer ligger i min lomme.
['miːnə pa'piːɐ̯ 'legʌ i min 'lʌmə]

Calm down!
Tag det roligt!
['tæˀ de 'ʁoːlit]

May I use your phone?
Må jeg bruge din telefon?
[mɔˀ ja 'bʁuːə din telə'foˀn?]

Call an ambulance!
Ring efter en ambulance!
['ʁɛŋə 'ɛftʌ en ambu'laŋsə]

It's urgent!
Det haster!
[de 'hastə]

It's an emergency!
Det er en nødsituation!
[de 'æɐ̯ en 'nød sitwa'ɕoˀn]

Please hurry up!
Vær sød at skynde dig!
['vɛɐ̯ˀ 'søðˀ ʌ 'skønə 'dɑj]

Would you please call a doctor?
Vil du venligst ringe til en læge?
['ve du 'vɛnlist 'ʁɛŋə te en 'lɛːjə?]

Where is the hospital?
Hvor er hospitalet?
[vɒˀ 'æɐ̯ hɒspi'tæˀləð?]

How are you feeling?
Hvordan har du det?
[vɒ'dan hɑˀ du de?]

Are you all right?
Er du okay?
[æɐ̯ du ɔw'kɛj?]

What's happened?
Hvad er der sket?
['vað 'æɐ̯ 'dɛˀɐ̯ 'skeˀð?]

I feel better now.	**Jeg har det bedre nu.** [ja haˀ de ˈbɛðʁʌ ˈnu]
It's OK.	**Det er OK.** [de ˈæɡ̊ ɔwˈkɛj]
It's all right.	**Det er OK.** [de ˈæɡ̊ ɔwˈkɛj]

At the pharmacy

pharmacy (drugstore)	**apotek** [apo'te²k]
24-hour pharmacy	**døgnåbent apotek** ['dʌj²n 'ɔ:bənt apo'te²k]
Where is the closest pharmacy?	**Hvor er det nærmeste apotek?** [vɒ² 'æɐ̯ de 'næɐ̯məstə apo'te²k?]

Is it open now?	**Holder det åbent nu?** ['hʌlʌ de 'ɔ:bənt 'nu?]
At what time does it open?	**Hvornår åbner det?** [vɒ'nɒ² 'ɔ:bnʌ de?]
At what time does it close?	**Hvornår lukker det?** [vɒ'nɒ² 'lɔkɐ̯ de?]

Is it far?	**Er det langt væk?** [æɐ̯ de 'laŋ²t vɛk?]
Can I get there on foot?	**Kan jeg komme derhen til fods?** ['kan² ja 'kʌmə 'dɛ²ɐ̯'hɛn te 'fo²ðs?]
Can you show me on the map?	**Kan du vise mig på kortet?** ['kan du 'vi:sə maj pɔ 'kɒ:təð?]

Please give me something for ...	**Kan du give mig noget for ...** ['kan du gi² maj 'no:əð fə ...]
a headache	**hovedpine** ['ho:əð,pi:nə]
a cough	**hoste** ['ho:stə]
a cold	**forkølelse** [fʌ'kø²ləlsə]
the flu	**influenza** [enflu'ɛnsa]

a fever	**feber** ['fe²bʌ]
a stomach ache	**ondt i maven** ['ɔnt i 'mæ:vən]
nausea	**kvalme** ['kvalmə]
diarrhea	**diarré** [dia'ʁɛ²]
constipation	**forstoppelse** [fʌ'stʌpəlsə]
pain in the back	**rygsmerter** ['ʁœg 'smæɐ̯tə]

chest pain	**brystsmerter** ['bʁœst 'smæɐ̯tə]
side stitch	**sidesting** ['si:ðə 'steŋˀ]
abdominal pain	**mavesmerter** ['mæːvə 'smæɐ̯tə]

pill	**pille** ['pelə]
ointment, cream	**salve, creme** ['salvə, 'kʁɛˀm]
syrup	**sirup** ['siˀʁɔp]
spray	**spray** ['spʁɛj]
drops	**dråber** ['dʁɔːbʌ]

You need to go to the hospital.	**Du er nødt til at tage på hospitalet.** [du 'æɐ̯ 'nøˀt te ʌ tæˀ pɔ hɔspi'tæˀləð]
health insurance	**sygesikring** ['syːə̯ˌsekʁɛŋ]
prescription	**recept** [ʁɛ'sɛpt]
insect repellant	**mygge-afskrækker** ['mygə-'ɑwˌskʁakʌ]
Band Aid	**hæfteplaster** ['hɛftə 'plastʌ]

The bare minimum

Excuse me, ...
Undskyld, ...
['ɔnˌskylʔ, ...]

Hello.
Hej.
['hɑj]

Thank you.
Tak.
[tɑk]

Good bye.
Farvel.
[fɑ'vɛl]

Yes.
Ja.
['jæ]

No.
Nej.
[nɑjʔ]

I don't know.
Jeg ved det ikke.
[jɑj ve de 'ekə]

Where? | Where to? | When?
Hvor? | Hvorhen? | Hvornår?
['vɒʔ? | 'vɒʔˌhɛn? | vɒ'nɒʔ?]

I need ...
Jeg har brug for ...
[jɑ hɑʔ 'bʁuʔ fə ...]

I want ...
Jeg vil ...
[jɑj ve ...]

Do you have ...?
Har du ...?
['hɑʔ du ...?]

Is there a ... here?
Er der en ... her?
[æɐ̯ 'dɛʔɐ̯ en ... hɛʔɐ̯?]

May I ...?
Må jeg ...?
[mɔʔ jɑ ...?]

..., please (polite request)
... venligst
[... 'vɛnlist]

I'm looking for ...
Jeg leder efter ...
[jɑ 'le:ðə 'ɛftʌ ...]

restroom
toilet
[toa'lɛt]

ATM
udbetalingsautomat
[uðʔbe'tæʔleŋs ɑwto'mæʔt]

pharmacy (drugstore)
apotek
[ɑpo'teʔk]

hospital
hospital
[hɔspi'tæʔl]

police station
politistation
[poli'ti sta'ɕoʔn]

subway
metro
['me:tʁo]

taxi	**taxi** ['tɑksi]
train station	**togstation** ['tɔw sta'ɕo'n]
My name is ...	**Mit navn er ...** [mit 'nɑw'n 'æɐ̯ ...]
What's your name?	**Hvad er dit navn?** ['vað 'æɐ̯ dit nɑw'n?]
Could you please help me?	**Kan du hjælpe mig?** ['kan du 'jɛlpə mɑj?]
I've got a problem.	**Jeg har fået et problem.** [jɑ hɑ' fɔ' et pʁo'ble'm]
I don't feel well.	**Jeg føler mig dårlig.** [jɑ 'fø:lɐ mɑj 'dɒ:li]
Call an ambulance!	**Ring efter en ambulance!** ['ʁɛŋə 'ɛftʌ en ɑmbu'lɑŋsə]
May I make a call?	**Må jeg foretage et opkald?** [mɔ' jɑ 'fɒ:ɒ̯tæ' et 'ʌpkal'?]
I'm sorry.	**Det er jeg ked af.** [de 'æɐ̯ jɑ 'keð' æ']
You're welcome.	**Selv tak.** [sɛl' tak]
I, me	**Jeg, mig** [jɑj, mɑj]
you (inform.)	**du** [du]
he	**han** [han]
she	**hun** [hun]
they (masc.)	**de** [di]
they (fem.)	**de** [di]
we	**vi** [vi]
you (pl)	**I, De** [I, di]
you (sg, form.)	**De** [di]
ENTRANCE	**INDGANG** ['en,gɑŋ']
EXIT	**UDGANG** ['uð,gɑŋ']
OUT OF ORDER	**UDE AF DRIFT** ['u:ðə æ' 'dʁɛft]
CLOSED	**LUKKET** ['lɔkəð]

OPEN	**ÅBEN** [ˈɔːbən]
FOR WOMEN	**TIL KVINDER** [te ˈkvenʌ]
FOR MEN	**TIL MÆND** [te ˈmɛnˀ]

T&P BOOKS

CONCISE DICTIONARY

This section contains more than 1,500 useful words arranged alphabetically. The dictionary includes a lot of gastronomic terms and will be helpful when ordering food at a restaurant or buying groceries

T&P Books Publishing

DICTIONARY CONTENTS

T&P Books Publishing

T&P Books Publishing

time	**tid** (f)	['tiðˀ]
hour	**time** (f)	['tiːmə]
half an hour	**en halv time**	[en 'halˀ 'tiːmə]
minute	**minut** (i)	[meˈnut]
second	**sekund** (i)	[seˈkɔnˀd]

today (adv)	**i dag**	[i 'dæˀ]
tomorrow (adv)	**i morgen**	[i 'mɒːɒn]
yesterday (adv)	**i går**	[i 'gɒˀ]

Monday	**mandag** (f)	['manˀda]
Tuesday	**tirsdag** (f)	['tiɐ̯ˀsda]
Wednesday	**onsdag** (f)	['ɔnˀsda]
Thursday	**torsdag** (f)	['tɒˀsda]
Friday	**fredag** (f)	['fʁɛˀda]
Saturday	**lørdag** (f)	['lœɐ̯da]
Sunday	**søndag** (f)	['sœnˀda]

day	**dag** (f)	['dæˀ]
working day	**arbejdsdag** (f)	['ɑːbɑjds‚dæˀ]
public holiday	**festdag** (f)	['fɛst‚dæˀ]
weekend	**weekend** (f)	['wiː‚kɛnd]

week	**uge** (f)	['uːə]
last week (adv)	**sidste uge**	[i 'sistə 'uːə]
next week (adv)	**i næste uge**	[i 'nɛstə 'uːə]

| sunrise | **solopgang** (f) | ['soːl 'ʌp‚gɑŋˀ] |
| sunset | **solnedgang** (f) | ['soːl 'neð‚gɑŋˀ] |

| in the morning | **om morgenen** | [ʌm 'mɒːɒnən] |
| in the afternoon | **om eftermiddagen** | [ʌm 'ɛftʌme‚dæˀən] |

| in the evening | **om aftenen** | [ʌm 'ɑftənən] |
| tonight (this evening) | **i aften** | [i 'ɑftən] |

| at night | **om natten** | [ʌm 'natən] |
| midnight | **midnat** (f) | ['miðˌnat] |

January	**januar** (f)	['janu‚ɑˀ]
February	**februar** (f)	['febʁu‚ɑˀ]
March	**marts** (f)	['mɑːts]
April	**april** (f)	[aˈpʁiˀl]
May	**maj** (f)	['mɑjˀ]
June	**juni** (f)	['juˀni]

July	juli (f)	[ˈjuˀli]
August	august (f)	[awˈɡɔst]
September	september (f)	[sepˈtɛmˀbʌ]
October	oktober (f)	[okˈtoˀbʌ]
November	november (f)	[noˈvɛmˀbʌ]
December	december (f)	[deˈsɛmˀbʌ]

in spring	om foråret	[ʌm ˈfɔːˌpˀð]
in summer	om sommeren	[ʌm ˈsʌmʌən]
in fall	om efteråret	[ʌm ˈɛftʌˌpˀð]
in winter	om vinteren	[ʌm ˈvenˀtʌən]

month	måned (f)	[ˈmɔːnəð]
season (summer, etc.)	årstid (f)	[ˈɔːsˌtið]
year	år (i)	[ˈɒ]
century	århundrede (i)	[ɒˈhunʁʌðə]

2. Numbers. Numerals

digit, figure	ciffer (i)	[ˈsifʌ]
number	tal (i)	[ˈtal]
minus sign	minus (i)	[ˈmiːnus]
plus sign	plus (i)	[ˈplus]
sum, total	sum (f)	[ˈsɔmˀ]

first (adj)	første	[ˈfœɐ̯stə]
second (adj)	anden	[ˈanən]
third (adj)	tredje	[ˈtʁɛðjə]

0 zero	nul	[ˈnɔl]
1 one	en	[ˈen]
2 two	to	[ˈtoˀ]
3 three	tre	[ˈtʁɛˀ]
4 four	fire	[ˈfiˀʌ]

5 five	fem	[ˈfɛmˀ]
6 six	seks	[ˈsɛks]
7 seven	syv	[ˈsywˀ]
8 eight	otte	[ˈɔːtə]
9 nine	ni	[ˈniˀ]
10 ten	ti	[ˈtiˀ]

11 eleven	elleve	[ˈɛlvə]
12 twelve	tolv	[ˈtʌlˀ]
13 thirteen	tretten	[ˈtʁatən]
14 fourteen	fjorten	[ˈfjoɐ̯tən]
15 fifteen	femten	[ˈfɛmtən]

| 16 sixteen | seksten | [ˈsɑjstən] |
| 17 seventeen | sytten | [ˈsøtən] |

| 18 eighteen | atten | ['atən] |
| 19 nineteen | nitten | ['netən] |

20 twenty	tyve	['ty:və]
30 thirty	tredive	['tʁaðvə]
40 forty	fyrre	['fœɐ̯ʌ]
50 fifty	halvtreds	[hal'tʁɛs]

60 sixty	tres	['tʁɛs]
70 seventy	halvfjerds	[hal'fjæɐ̯s]
80 eighty	firs	['fiɐ̯'s]
90 ninety	halvfems	[hal'fɛmˀs]

100 one hundred	hundrede	['hunʌðə]
200 two hundred	tohundrede	['tɔwˌhunʌðə]
300 three hundred	trehundrede	['tʁɛˌhunʌðə]
400 four hundred	firehundrede	['fiɐ̯ˌhunʌðə]
500 five hundred	femhundrede	['fɛmˌhunʌðə]

600 six hundred	sekshundrede	['sɛksˌhunʌðə]
700 seven hundred	syvhundrede	['sywˌhunʌðə]
800 eight hundred	ottehundrede	['ɔːtəˌhunʌðə]
900 nine hundred	nihundrede	['niˌhunʌðə]
1000 one thousand	tusind	['tuˀsən]

| 10000 ten thousand | titusind | ['tiˌtuˀsən] |
| one hundred thousand | hundredetusind | ['hunʌðəˌtuˀsən] |

| million | million (f) | [mili'oˀn] |
| billion | milliard (f) | [mili'ɑˀd] |

3. Humans. Family

man (adult male)	mand (f)	['manˀ]
young man	ung mand, yngling (f)	['ɔŋ manˀ], ['øŋleŋ]
teenager	teenager (f)	['tiːnˌɛjtɕʌ]
woman	kvinde (f)	['kvenə]
girl (young woman)	pige (f)	['piːə]

age	alder (f)	['alˀʌ]
adult (adj)	voksen	['vʌksən]
middle-aged (adj)	midaldrende	['miðˌalˀʁʌnə]
elderly (adj)	ældre	['ɛldʁʌ]
old (adj)	gammel	['gaməl]

old man	gammel mand (f)	['gaməl 'manˀ]
old woman	gammel dame (f)	['gaməl 'dæːmə]
retirement	pension (f)	[paŋ'ɕoˀn]
to retire (from job)	at gå på pension	[ʌ gɔˀ pɔ paŋ'ɕoˀn]
retiree	pensionist (f)	[paŋɕo'nist]

mother	mor (f), moder (f)	['moɐ̯], ['moːðʌ]
father	far (f), fader (f)	['faː], ['fæːðʌ]
son	søn (f)	['sœn]
daughter	datter (f)	['datʌ]
brother	bror (f)	['bʁoɐ̯]
elder brother	storebror (f)	['stoɐ̯ˌbʁoɐ̯]
younger brother	lillebror (f)	['liləˌbʁoɐ̯]
sister	søster (f)	['søstʌ]
elder sister	storesøster (f)	['stoɐ̯ˌsøstʌ]
younger sister	lillesøster (f)	['liləˌsøstʌ]
parents	forældre (pl)	[fʌˈɛlʔdʁʌ]
child	barn (i)	['baʔn]
children	børn (pl)	['bœɐ̯ʔn]
stepmother	stedmor (f)	['stɛðˌmoɐ̯]
stepfather	stedfar (f)	['stɛðˌfaː]
grandmother	bedstemor (f)	['bɛstəˌmoɐ̯]
grandfather	bedstefar (f)	['bɛstəˌfaː]
grandson	barnebarn (i)	['baːnəˌbaʔn]
granddaughter	barnebarn (i)	['baːnəˌbaʔn]
grandchildren	børnebørn (pl)	['bœɐ̯nəˌbœɐ̯ʔn]
uncle	onkel (f)	['ɔŋʔkəl]
aunt	tante (f)	['tantə]
nephew	nevø (f)	[neˈvø]
niece	niece (f)	[niˈɛːsə]
wife	kone (f)	['koːnə]
husband	mand (f)	['manʔ]
married (masc.)	gift	['gift]
married (fem.)	gift	['gift]
widow	enke (f)	['ɛŋkə]
widower	enkemand (f)	['ɛŋkəˌmanʔ]
name (first name)	navn (i)	['nawʔn]
surname (last name)	efternavn (i)	['ɛftʌˌnawʔn]
relative	slægtning (f)	['slɛgtnen]
friend (masc.)	ven (f)	['vɛn]
friendship	venskab (i)	['vɛnˌskæʔb]
partner	partner (f)	['paːtnʌ]
superior (n)	overordnet (f)	['ɒwʌˌɒʔdnəð]
colleague	kollega (f)	[koˈleːga]
neighbors	naboer (pl)	['næːboʔʌ]

4. Human body

| organism (body) | organisme (f) | [ɒgaˈnismə] |
| body | krop (f) | ['kʁʌp] |

heart	**hjerte** (i)	['jæɐ̯tə]
blood	**blod** (i)	['bloˀð]
brain	**hjerne** (f)	['jæɐ̯nə]
nerve	**nerve** (f)	['næɐ̯və]
bone	**ben** (i)	['beˀn]
skeleton	**skelet** (i)	[skeˈlɛt]
spine (backbone)	**rygrad** (f)	['ʁœgˌʁɑˀð]
rib	**ribben** (i)	['ʁiˌbeˀn]
skull	**hovedskal** (f)	['hoːəðˌskalˀ]
muscle	**muskel** (f)	['muskəl]
lungs	**lunger** (f pl)	['loŋʌ]
skin	**hud** (f)	['huðˀ]
head	**hoved** (i)	['hoːəð]
face	**ansigt** (i)	['ansegt]
nose	**næse** (f)	['nɛːsə]
forehead	**pande** (f)	['panə]
cheek	**kind** (f)	['kenˀ]
mouth	**mund** (f)	['mɔnˀ]
tongue	**tunge** (f)	['toŋə]
tooth	**tand** (f)	['tanˀ]
lips	**læber** (f pl)	['lɛːbʌ]
chin	**hage** (f)	['hæːjə]
ear	**øre** (i)	['øːʌ]
neck	**hals** (f)	['halˀs]
throat	**strube, hals** (f)	['stʁuːbə], ['halˀs]
eye	**øje** (i)	['ʌjə]
pupil	**pupil** (f)	[puˈpilˀ]
eyebrow	**øjenbryn** (i)	['ʌjənˌbʁyˀn]
eyelash	**øjenvippe** (f)	['ʌjənˌvepə]
hair	**hår** (i pl)	['hɒˀ]
hairstyle	**frisure** (f)	[fʁiˈsyˀʌ]
mustache	**moustache** (f)	[muˈstæːɕ]
beard	**skæg** (i)	['skɛˀg]
to have (a beard, etc.)	**at have**	[ʌ 'hæːvə]
bald (adj)	**skaldet**	['skaləð]
hand	**hånd** (f)	['hʌnˀ]
arm	**arm** (f)	['ɑˀm]
finger	**finger** (f)	['feŋˀʌ]
nail	**negl** (f)	['najˀl]
palm	**håndflade** (f)	['hʌnˌflæːðə]
shoulder	**skulder** (f)	['skulʌ]
leg	**ben** (i)	['beˀn]
foot	**fod** (f)	['foˀð]

| knee | knæ (i) | ['knɛˀ] |
| heel | hæl (f) | ['hɛˀl] |

back	ryg (f)	['ʁœg]
waist	midje, talje (f)	['miðjə], ['taljə]
beauty mark	skønhedsplet (f)	['skœnheðsˌplɛt]
birthmark	modermærke (i)	['moːðʌ'mæɐ̯kə]
(café au lait spot)		

5. Medicine. Diseases. Drugs

health	helse, sundhed (f)	['hɛlsə], ['sɔnˌheð']
well (not sick)	frisk	['fʁɛsk]
sickness	sygdom (f)	['syːˌdʌmˀ]
to be sick	at være syg	[ʌ 'vɛːʌ syˀ]
ill, sick (adj)	syg	['syˀ]

cold (illness)	forkølelse (f)	[fʌ'køˀləlsə]
to catch a cold	at blive forkølet	[ʌ 'bliːə fʌ'køˀləð]
tonsillitis	angina (f)	[ɑn'giːna]
pneumonia	lungebetændelse (f)	['loŋə be'tɛnˀəlsə]
flu, influenza	influenza (f)	[ɛnflu'ɛnsa]

runny nose (coryza)	snue (f)	['snuːə]
cough	hoste (f)	['hoːstə]
to cough (vi)	at hoste	[ʌ 'hoːstə]
to sneeze (vi)	at nyse	[ʌ 'nyːsə]

stroke	hjerneblødning (f)	['jæɐ̯nəˌbløðnen]
heart attack	infarkt (i, f)	[en'fɑːkt]
allergy	allergi (f)	[alæɐ̯'giˀ]
asthma	astma (f)	['astma]
diabetes	diabetes (f)	[dia'beːtəs]

tumor	svulst, tumor (f)	['svulˀst], ['tuːmɒ]
cancer	kræft (f), cancer (f)	['kʁaft], ['kanˀsʌ]
alcoholism	alkoholisme (f)	[alkoho'lismə]
AIDS	AIDS (f)	['ɛjds]
fever	feber (f)	['feˀbʌ]
seasickness	søsyge (f)	['søˌsyːə]

bruise (hématome)	blåt mærke (i)	['blʌt 'mæɐ̯kə]
bump (lump)	bule (f)	['buːlə]
to limp (vi)	at halte	[ʌ 'haltə]
dislocation	forvridning (f)	[fʌ'vʁiðˀnen]
to dislocate (vt)	at forvride	[ʌ fʌ'vʁiðˀə]

fracture	brud (i), fraktur (f)	['bʁuð], [fʁak'tuɐ̯ˀ]
burn (injury)	brandsår (i)	['bʁanˌsɒˀ]
injury	skade (f)	['skæːðə]

pain, ache	smerte (f)	['smæɐ̯tə]
toothache	tandpine (f)	['tanˌpiːnə]
to sweat (perspire)	at svede	[ʌ 'sveːðə]
deaf (adj)	døv	['døʔw]
mute (adj)	stum	['stɔmʔ]
immunity	immunitet (f)	[imuni'teʔt]
virus	virus (i, f)	['viːʁus]
microbe	mikrobe (f)	[mi'kʁoːbə]
bacterium	bakterie (f)	[bɑk'teɐ̯ʔiə]
infection	infektion (f)	[enfɛk'ɕoʔn]
hospital	sygehus (i)	['syːəˌhuʔs]
cure	kur, behandling (f)	['kuɐ̯ʔ], [be'hanʔleŋ]
to vaccinate (vt)	at vaccinere	[ʌ vɑksi'neʔʌ]
to be in a coma	at ligge i koma	[ʌ 'legə i 'koːma]
intensive care	intensivafdeling (f)	['entənˌsiwʔ 'ɑwˌdeʔleŋ]
symptom	symptom (i)	[sym'toʔm]
pulse	puls (f)	['pulʔs]

6. Feelings. Emotions. Conversation

I, me	jeg	['jɑj]
you	du	[du]
he	han	['han]
she	hun	['hun]
it	den, det	['dən], [de]
we	vi	['vi]
you (to a group)	I	[i]
they	de	['di]
Hello! (fam.)	Hej!	['hɑj]
Hello! (form.)	Hallo! Goddag!	[ha'lo], [go'dæʔ]
Good morning!	Godmorgen!	[go'mɒːɒn]
Good afternoon!	Goddag!	[go'dæʔ]
Good evening!	Godaften!	[go'ɑftən]
to say hello	at hilse	[ʌ 'hilsə]
to greet (vt)	at hilse	[ʌ 'hilsə]
How are you? (form.)	Hvordan har De det?	[vɒ'dan ha di de]
How are you? (fam.)	Hvordan går det?	[vɒ'dan gɒ: de]
Goodbye! (form.)	Farvel!	[fɑ'vɛl]
Bye! (fam.)	Hej hej!	['hɑj 'hɑj]
Thank you!	Tak!	['tɑk]
feelings	følelser (f pl)	['føːləlsʌ]
to be hungry	at være sulten	[ʌ 'vɛːʌ 'sultən]
to be thirsty	at være tørstig	[ʌ 'vɛːʌ 'tœɐ̯sti]

tired (adj)	træt	['tʁat]
to be worried	at bekymre sig	[ʌ be'køm'ʁʌ saj]
to be nervous	at være nervøs	[ʌ 'vɛːʌ næɡ'vøˀs]
hope	håb (i)	['hɔˀb]
to hope (vi, vt)	at håbe	[ʌ 'hɔːbə]

character	karakter (f)	[kɑɑk'teˀɡ]
modest (adj)	beskeden	[be'skeˀðən]
lazy (adj)	doven	['dɒwən]
generous (adj)	generøs	[ɕenə'ʁœˀs]
talented (adj)	talentfuld	[ta'lɛntˌfulˀ]

honest (adj)	ærlig	['æɐli]
serious (adj)	alvorlig	[al'voˀli]
shy, timid (adj)	forsagthed, genert	[ɕe'neɡ'tˌheðˀ], [ɕe'neɡˀt]
sincere (adj)	oprigtig	[ʌp'ʁɛgti]
coward	kryster (f)	['kʁystʌ]

to sleep (vi)	at sove	[ʌ 'sɒwə]
dream	drøm (f)	['dʁœmˀ]
bed	seng (f)	['sɛŋˀ]
pillow	pude (f)	['puːðə]

insomnia	søvnløshed (f)	['sœwnløsˌheðˀ]
to go to bed	at gå i seng	[ʌ 'gɔˀ i 'sɛŋˀ]
nightmare	mareridt (i)	['mɑːɑˌʁit]
alarm clock	vækkeur (i)	['vɛkəˌuɡˀ]

smile	smil (i)	['smiˀl]
to smile (vi)	at smile	[ʌ 'smiːlə]
to laugh (vi)	at le, at grine	[ʌ 'leˀ], [ʌ 'gʁiːnə]

quarrel	skænderi (i)	[skɛnʌ'ʁiˀ]
insult	fornærmelse (f)	[fʌ'næɡˀməlsə]
resentment	fornærmelse (f)	[fʌ'næɡˀməlsə]
angry (mad)	vred	['vʁɛðˀ]

7. Clothing. Personal accessories

clothes	tøj (i), klæder (i pl)	['tʌj], ['klɛːðʌ]
coat (overcoat)	frakke (f)	['fʁakə]
fur coat	pels (f), pelskåbe (f)	['pɛlˀs], ['pɛlsˌkɔːbə]
jacket (e.g., leather ~)	jakke (f)	['jakə]
raincoat (trenchcoat, etc.)	regnfrakke (f)	['ʁajnˌfʁakə]

shirt (button shirt)	skjorte (f)	['skjoɡtə]
pants	bukser (pl)	['boksʌ]
suit jacket	jakke (f)	['jakə]
suit	jakkesæt (i)	['jakəˌsɛt]
dress (frock)	kjole (f)	['kjoːlə]

skirt	nederdel (f)	['neðʌˌde'l]
T-shirt	t-shirt (f)	['tiːˌɕœːt]
bathrobe	badekåbe (f)	['bæːðəˌkɔːbə]
pajamas	pyjamas (f)	[py'jæːmas]
workwear	arbejdstøj (i)	['aːbɑjdsˌtʌj]

underwear	undertøj (i)	['ɔnʌˌtʌj]
socks	sokker (f pl)	['sʌkʌ]
bra	bh (f), brystholder (f)	[be'hɔ'], ['bʁœstˌhʌl'ʌ]
pantyhose	strømpebukser (pl)	['stʁœmbəˌboksʌ]
stockings (thigh highs)	strømper (f pl)	['stʁœmpʌ]
bathing suit	badedragt (f)	['bæːðəˌdʁɑgt]

hat	hue (f)	['huːə]
footwear	sko (f)	['sko']
boots (e.g., cowboy ~)	støvler (f pl)	['stœwlʌ]
heel	hæl (f)	['hɛ'l]

| shoestring | snøre (f) | ['snœːʌ] |
| shoe polish | skocreme (f) | ['skoˌkʁɛ'm] |

cotton (n)	bomuld (i, f)	['bʌˌmul']
wool (n)	uld (f)	['ul']
fur (n)	pels (f)	['pɛl's]

gloves	handsker (f pl)	['hanskʌ]
mittens	vanter (f pl)	['van'tʌ]
scarf (muffler)	halstørklæde (i)	['hals 'tœʁˌklɛːðə]

| glasses (eyeglasses) | briller (pl) | ['bʁɛlʌ] |
| umbrella | paraply (f) | [paɑ'ply'] |

| tie (necktie) | slips (i) | ['sleps] |
| handkerchief | lommetørklæde (i) | ['lʌməˌtœʁklɛːðə] |

| comb | kam (f) | ['kɑm'] |
| hairbrush | hårbørste (f) | ['hɔˌbœʁstə] |

buckle	spænde (i)	['spɛnə]
belt	bælte (i)	['bɛltə]
purse	dametaske (f)	['dæːmeˌtaskə]

| collar | krave (f) | ['kʁɑːvə] |
| pocket | lomme (f) | ['lʌmə] |

| sleeve | ærme (i) | ['æemə] |
| fly (on trousers) | gylp (f) | ['gyl'p] |

zipper (fastener)	lynlås (f)	['lynˌlɔ's]
button	knap (f)	['knɑp]
to get dirty (vi)	at smudse sig til	[ʌ 'smusə sɑ 'tel]
stain (mark, spot)	plet (f)	['plɛt]

8. City. Urban institutions

store	forretning (f), butik (f)	[fʌ'ʁatneŋ], [bu'tik]
shopping mall	indkøbscenter (i)	['en̩kø²bs ˌsɛn²tʌ]
supermarket	supermarked (i)	['suˀpʌˌmɑːkəð]
shoe store	skotøjsforretning (f)	['skoˌtʌjs fʌ'ʁatneŋ]
bookstore	boghandel (f)	['bɔwˌhanˀəl]

drugstore, pharmacy	apotek (i)	[ɑpo'teˀk]
bakery	bageri (i)	[bæjʌ'ʁiˀ]
pastry shop	konditori (i)	[kʌnditʌ'ʁiˀ]
grocery store	købmandsbutik (f)	['kømans bu'tik]
butcher shop	slagterbutik (f)	['slɑgtʌ bu'tik]
produce store	grønthandel (f)	['gʁœntˌhanˀəl]
market	marked (i)	['mɑːkəð]

hair salon	frisørsalon (f)	[fʁi'søʁ̩ saˌlʌŋ]
post office	postkontor (i)	['pʌst kɔn'toˀɐ̯]
dry cleaners	renseri (i)	[ʁansʌ'ʁiˀ]
circus	cirkus (i)	['siɐ̯kus]
zoo	zoologisk have (f)	[soo'loˀisk 'hæːvə]

theater	teater (i)	[te'æˀtʌ]
movie theater	biograf (f)	[bio'gʁɑˀf]
museum	museum (i)	[mu'sɛːɔm]
library	bibliotek (i)	[biblio'teˀk]

mosque	moske (f)	[mo'skeˀ]
synagogue	synagoge (f)	[syna'goːə]
cathedral	katedral (f)	[katə'dʁɑˀl]
temple	tempel (i)	['tɛmˀpəl]
church	kirke (f)	['kiɐ̯kə]

college	institut (i)	[ensdi'tut]
university	universitet (i)	[univæɐ̯si'teˀt]
school	skole (f)	['skoːlə]

hotel	hotel (i)	[ho'tɛlˀ]
bank	bank (f)	['baŋˀk]
embassy	ambassade (f)	[ɑmba'sæːðə]
travel agency	rejsebureau (i)	['ʁɑjsə byˌʁo]

subway	metro (f)	['meːtʁo]
hospital	sygehus (i)	['syːəˌhuˀs]
gas station	tankstation (f)	['taŋk sta'ɕˀon]
parking lot	parkeringsplads (f)	[pɑ'keˀɐ̯eŋsˌplas]

ENTRANCE	INDGANG	['enˌgɑŋˀ]
EXIT	UDGANG	['uðˌgɑŋˀ]
PUSH	TRYK	['tʁœk]
PULL	TRÆK	['tʁak]

| OPEN | **ÅBENT** | ['ɔːbənt] |
| CLOSED | **LUKKET** | ['lɔkəð] |

monument	**monument** (i)	[monu'mɛnˀt]
fortress	**fæstning** (f)	['fɛstnɛŋ]
palace	**palads** (i)	[pa'las]

medieval (adj)	**middelalderlig**	['miðəlˌalˀʌli]
ancient (adj)	**gammel**	['gaməl]
national (adj)	**national**	[naɕo'næˀl]
famous (monument, etc.)	**kendt, berømt**	['kɛnˀt], [be'ʁœmˀt]

9. Money. Finances

money	**penge** (pl)	['pɛŋə]
coin	**mønt** (f)	['mønˀt]
dollar	**dollar** (f)	['dʌlʌ]
euro	**euro** (f)	['œwʁo]

ATM	**pengeautomat** (f)	['pɛŋə awto'mæˀt]
currency exchange	**vekselkontor** (i)	['vɛksəl kɔn'toˀɡ]
exchange rate	**kurs** (f)	['kuɡˀs]
cash	**kontanter** (pl)	[kɔn'tanˀtʌ]

How much?	**Hvor meget?**	[vɒˀ 'maɑð]
to pay (vi, vt)	**at betale**	[ʌ be'tæˀlə]
payment	**betaling** (f)	[be'tæˀlɛŋ]
change (give the ~)	**byttepenge** (pl)	['bytəˌpɛŋə]

price	**pris** (f)	['pʁiˀs]
discount	**rabat** (f)	[ʁa'bat]
cheap (adj)	**billig**	['bili]
expensive (adj)	**dyr**	['dyɡˀ]

bank	**bank** (f)	['baŋˀk]
account	**konto** (f)	['kʌnto]
credit card	**kreditkort** (i)	[kʁɛ'dit kɔːt]
check	**check** (f)	['ɕɛk]
to write a check	**at skrive en check**	[ʌ 'skʁiːvə en 'ɕɛk]
checkbook	**checkhæfte** (i)	['ɕɛkˌhɛftə]

debt	**gæld** (f)	['gɛlˀ]
debtor	**skyldner** (f)	['skylnʌ]
to lend (money)	**at låne ud**	[ʌ 'lɔːnə ˌuðˀ]
to borrow (vi, vt)	**at låne**	[ʌ 'lɔːnə]

to rent (~ a tuxedo)	**at leje**	[ʌ 'lɑjə]
on credit (adv)	**på kredit**	[pɔ kʁɛ'dit]
wallet	**tegnebog** (f)	['tajnəˌbɔˀw]
safe	**pengeskab** (i)	['pɛŋəˌskæˀb]

| inheritance | arv (f) | ['ɑˀw] |
| fortune (wealth) | formue (f) | ['foːˌmuːə] |

tax	skat (f)	['skat]
fine	bøde (f)	['bøːðə]
to fine (vt)	at give bødestraf	[ʌ 'giˀ 'bøːðəˌstʁaf]

wholesale (adj)	engros-	[ɑŋ'gʁo-]
retail (adj)	detail-	[de'tajl-]
to insure (vt)	at forsikre	[ʌ fʌ'sekʁʌ]
insurance	forsikring (f)	[fʌ'sekʁɛŋ]

capital	kapital (f)	[kapi'tæˀl]
turnover	omsætning (f)	['ʌmˌsɛtnen]
stock (share)	aktie (f)	['akɕə]
profit	profit, fortjeneste (f)	[pʁo'fit], [fʌ'tjɛˀnəstə]
profitable (adj)	profitabel	[pʁofi'tæˀbəl]

crisis	krise (f)	['kʁiˀsə]
bankruptcy	konkurs (f)	[kʌŋ'kuɡˀs]
to go bankrupt	at gå konkurs	[ʌ 'gɔˀ kʌŋ'kuɡˀs]

accountant	bogholder (f)	['bowˌhʌlʌ]
salary	løn (f)	['lœnˀ]
bonus (money)	bonus (f), gratiale (i)	['boːnus], [gʁati'æːlə]

10. Transportation

bus	bus (f)	['bus]
streetcar	sporvogn (f)	['spoɡˌvowˀn]
trolley bus	trolleybus (f)	['tʁʌliˌbus]

to go by ...	at køre på ...	[ʌ 'køːʌ 'pɔˀ ...]
to get on (~ the bus)	at stå på ...	[ʌ stɔˀ 'pɔˀ ...]
to get off ...	at stå af ...	[ʌ stɔˀ 'æˀ ...]

stop (e.g., bus ~)	stop, stoppested (i)	['stʌp], ['stʌpəstɛð]
terminus	endestation (f)	['ɛnəsta'ɕoˀn]
schedule	køreplan (f)	['køːʌˌplæˀn]
ticket	billet (f)	[bi'lɛt]
to be late (for ...)	at komme for sent	[ʌ 'kʌmə fʌ 'seˀnt]

taxi, cab	taxi (f)	['taksi]
by taxi	i taxi	[i 'taksi]
taxi stand	taxiholdeplads (f)	['taksi 'hʌləˌplas]

traffic	trafik (f)	[tʁa'fik]
rush hour	myldretid (f)	['mylʁʌˌtiðˀ]
to park (vi)	at parkere	[ʌ pa'keˀʌ]
subway	metro (f)	['meːtʁo]

station	**station** (f)	[sta'ɕoˀn]
train	**tog** (i)	['toˀw]
train station	**banegård** (f)	['bæːnəˌgɒˀ]
rails	**skinner** (f pl)	['skenʌ]
compartment	**kupe, kupé** (f)	[ku'peˀ]
berth	**køje** (f)	['kʌjə]

airplane	**fly** (i)	['flyˀ]
air ticket	**flybillet** (f)	['fly bi'lɛt]
airline	**flyselskab** (i)	['flyˀsɛlˌskæˀb]
airport	**lufthavn** (f)	['lɔftˌhɑwˀn]

flight (act of flying)	**flyvning** (f)	['flywneŋ]
luggage	**bagage** (f)	[ba'gæːɕə]
luggage cart	**bagagevogn** (f)	[ba'gæːɕəˌvɒwˀn]

ship	**skib** (i)	['skiˀb]
cruise ship	**cruiseskib** (i)	['kʁuːsˌskiˀb]
yacht	**yacht** (f)	['jagt]
boat (flat-bottomed ~)	**båd** (f)	['bɔˀð]

captain	**kaptajn** (f)	[kap'tajˀn]
cabin	**kahyt** (f)	[ka'hyt]
port (harbor)	**havn** (f)	['hɑwˀn]

bicycle	**cykel** (f)	['sykəl]
scooter	**scooter** (f)	['skuːtʌ]
motorcycle, bike	**motorcykel** (f)	['moːtʌˌsykəl]
pedal	**pedal** (f)	[pe'dæˀl]
pump	**pumpe** (f)	['pɔmpə]
wheel	**hjul** (i)	['juˀl]

automobile, car	**bil** (f)	['biˀl]
ambulance	**ambulance** (f)	[ambu'laŋsə]
truck	**lastbil** (f)	['lastˌbiˀl]
used (adj)	**brugt**	['bʁɔgt]
car crash	**bilulykke** (f)	['bil 'uˌløkə]
repair	**reparation** (f)	[ʁɛpʁɑ'ɕoˀn]

11. Food. Part 1

meat	**kød** (i)	['køð]
chicken	**høne** (f)	['hœːnə]
duck	**and** (f)	['anˀ]
pork	**flæsk** (i)	['flɛsk]
veal	**kalvekød** (i)	['kalvəˌkøð]
lamb	**lammekød** (i)	['laməˌkøð]
beef	**oksekød** (i)	['ʌksəˌkøð]
sausage (bologna, pepperoni, etc.)	**pølse** (f)	['pølsə]

egg	æg (i)	['ɛˀg]
fish	fisk (f)	['fesk]
cheese	ost (f)	['ɔst]
sugar	sukker (i)	['sɔkʌ]
salt	salt (i)	['salˀt]

rice	ris (f)	['ʁiˀs]
pasta (macaroni)	pasta (f)	['pasta]
butter	smør (i)	['smœʁ]
vegetable oil	vegetabilsk olie (f)	[vegeta'biˀlsk 'oljə]
bread	brød (i)	['bʁœðˀ]
chocolate (n)	chokolade (f)	[ɕoko'læːðə]

wine	vin (f)	['viˀn]
coffee	kaffe (f)	['kɑfə]
milk	mælk (f)	['mɛlˀk]
juice	juice (f)	['dʒuːs]

| beer | øl (i) | ['øl] |
| tea | te (f) | ['teˀ] |

tomato	tomat (f)	[to'mæˀt]
cucumber	agurk (f)	[a'guʁk]
carrot	gulerod (f)	['gulə,ʁoˀð]
potato	kartoffel (f)	[kɑ'tʌfəl]

| onion | løg (i) | ['lʌjˀ] |
| garlic | hvidløg (i) | ['við,lʌjˀ] |

cabbage	kål (f)	['kɔˀl]
beetroot	rødbede (f)	[ʁœð'beːðə]
eggplant	aubergine (f)	[obæʁ'ɕiːn]
dill	dild (f)	['dilˀ]

| lettuce | salat (f) | [sa'læˀt] |
| corn (maize) | majs (f) | ['mɑjˀs] |

fruit	frugt (f)	['fʁɔgt]
apple	æble (i)	['ɛˀble]
pear	pære (f)	['pɛˀʌ]
lemon	citron (f)	[si'tʁoˀn]

| orange | appelsin (f) | [ɑpəl'siˀn] |
| strawberry (garden ~) | jordbær (i) | ['joʁ,bæʁ] |

plum	blomme (f)	['blʌmə]
raspberry	hindbær (i)	['hen,bæʁ]
pineapple	ananas (f)	['ananas]
banana	banan (f)	[ba'næˀn]
watermelon	vandmelon (f)	['van me'loˀn]
grape	drue (f)	['dʁuːə]
melon	melon (f)	[me'loˀn]

12. Food. Part 2

cuisine	**køkken** (i)	['køkən]
recipe	**opskrift** (f)	['ʌpˌskʁɛft]
food	**mad** (f)	['mað]
to have breakfast	**at spise morgenmad**	[ʌ 'spiːsə 'mɒːɒnˌmað]
to have lunch	**at spise frokost**	[ʌ 'spiːsə 'fʁɔkʌst]
to have dinner	**at spise aftensmad**	[ʌ 'spiːsə 'ɑftənsˌmað]
taste, flavor	**smag** (f)	['smæʔj]
tasty (adj)	**lækker**	['lɛkʌ]
cold (adj)	**kold**	['kʌlʔ]
hot (adj)	**hed, varm**	['heðʔ], ['vɑʔm]
sweet (sugary)	**sød**	['søðʔ]
salty (adj)	**saltet**	['saltəð]
sandwich (bread)	**smørrebrød** (i)	['smœɐ̯ʌˌbʁœðʔ]
side dish	**tilbehør** (i)	['telbeˌhøʔɐ̯]
filling (for cake, pie)	**fyld** (i, f)	['fylʔ]
sauce	**sovs, sauce** (f)	['sɒwʔs]
piece (of cake, pie)	**stykke** (i)	['støkə]
diet	**diæt** (f)	[di'ɛʔt]
vitamin	**vitamin** (i)	[vita'miʔn]
calorie	**kalorie** (f)	[ka'loɐ̯ʔjə]
vegetarian (n)	**vegetar, vegetarianer** (f)	[vegə'taʔ], [vegətai'æʔnʌ]
restaurant	**restaurant** (f)	[ʁɛsto'ʁɑn]
coffee house	**cafe, kaffebar** (f)	[ka'feʔ], ['kɑfəˌbaʔ]
appetite	**appetit** (f)	[apə'tit]
Enjoy your meal!	**Velbekomme!**	['vɛlbə'kʌmʔə]
waiter	**tjener** (f)	['tjɛːnʌ]
waitress	**servitrice** (f)	[sæɐ̯vi'tʁiːsə]
bartender	**bartender** (f)	['bɑːˌtɛndʌ]
menu	**menu** (f)	[me'ny]
spoon	**ske** (f)	['skeʔ]
knife	**kniv** (f)	['kniwʔ]
fork	**gaffel** (f)	['gɑfəl]
cup (e.g., coffee ~)	**kop** (f)	['kʌp]
plate (dinner ~)	**tallerken** (f)	[ta'læɐ̯kən]
saucer	**underkop** (f)	['ɔnʌˌkʌp]
napkin (on table)	**serviet** (f)	[sæɐ̯vi'ɛt]
toothpick	**tandstikker** (f)	['tanˌstekʌ]
to order (meal)	**at bestille**	[ʌ be'stelʔə]
course, dish	**ret** (f)	['ʁat]
portion	**portion** (f)	[pɒ'ɕoʔn]

appetizer	forret (f)	['fɔːʁat]
salad	salat (f)	[sa'læ'tˀ]
soup	suppe (f)	['sɔpə]

dessert	dessert (f)	[de'sɛɡˀt]
jam (whole fruit jam)	syltetøj (i)	['syltəˌtʌj]
ice-cream	is (f)	['iˀs]

check	regning (f)	['ʁajneŋ]
to pay the check	at betale regningen	[ʌ be'tæˀlə 'ʁajneŋən]
tip	drikkepenge (pl)	['dʁɛkəˌpɛŋə]

13. House. Apartment. Part 1

house	hus (i)	['huˀs]
country house	fritidshus (i)	['fʁitiðsˌhuˀs]
villa (seaside ~)	villa (f)	['vila]

floor, story	etage (f)	[e'tæˀɕə]
entrance	indgang (f)	['enˌgaŋˀ]
wall	mur (f), væg (f)	['muɡˀ], ['vɛˀg]
roof	tag (i)	['tæˀj]
chimney	skorsten (f)	['skɒːˌsteˀn]

attic (storage place)	loft (i)	['lʌft]
window	vindue (i)	['vendu]
window ledge	vindueskarm (f)	['vendusˌkɑˀm]
balcony	balkon, altan (f)	[bal'kʌŋ], [al'tæˀn]

stairs (stairway)	trappe (f)	['tʁɑpə]
mailbox	postkasse (f)	['pʌstˌkasə]
garbage can	skraldebøtte (f)	['skʁɑləˌbøtə]
elevator	elevator (f)	[elə'væːtʌ]

electricity	elektricitet (f)	[elɛktʁisi'teˀt]
light bulb	elpære (f)	['ɛlˌpɛˀʌ]
switch	afbryder (f)	['awˌbʁyðˀʌ]
wall socket	stikkontakt (f)	['stek kɔn'takt]
fuse	sikring (f)	['sekʁɛŋ]

door	dør (f)	['dœˀɡ]
handle, doorknob	dørhåndtag (i)	['dœɡˌhʌnˀˌtæˀj]
key	nøgle (f)	['nʌjlə]
doormat	dørmåtte (f)	['dœɡˌmʌtə]

door lock	dørlås (f)	['dœɡˌlɔˀs]
doorbell	ringeklokke (f)	['ʁɛŋəˌklʌkə]
knock (at the door)	banker (f pl)	['baŋkʌ]
to knock (vi)	at banke	[ʌ 'baŋkə]
peephole	kighul (i)	['kigˌhɔl]

yard	**gård** (f)	['gɒˀ]
garden	**have** (f)	['hæːvə]
swimming pool	**svømmebassin** (i)	['svœməbaˌsɛŋ]
gym (home gym)	**gym** (i)	['dʒyːmˀ]
tennis court	**tennisbane** (f)	['tɛnisˌbæːnə]
garage	**garage** (f)	[ga'ʁɑːɕə]
private property	**privat ejendom** (f)	[pʁi'væˀt 'ɑjənˌdʌmˀ]
warning sign	**advarselsskilt** (i)	['aðˌvɑːsəls 'skelˀt]
security	**sikkerhed** (f)	['sekʌˌheðˀ]
security guard	**sikkerhedsvagt** (f)	['sekʌˌheðs 'vɑgt]
renovations	**renovering** (f)	[ʁɛno've'ɐ̯ən]
to renovate (vt)	**at renovere**	[ʌ ʁɛno've'ʌ]
to put in order	**at bringe orden**	[ʌ 'bʁɛŋə 'ɒˀdən]
to paint (~ a wall)	**at male**	[ʌ 'mæːlə]
wallpaper	**tapet** (i)	[ta'peˀt]
to varnish (vt)	**at lakere**	[ʌ la'keˀʌ]
pipe	**rør** (i)	['ʁœˀɐ̯]
tools	**værktøjer** (i pl)	['væɐ̯kˌtʌjʌ]
basement	**kælder** (f)	['kɛlʌ]
sewerage (system)	**afløb** (i)	['ɑwˌløˀb]

14. House. Apartment. Part 2

apartment	**lejlighed** (f)	['lɑjliˌheðˀ]
room	**rum, værelse** (i)	['ʁɒmˀ], ['væɐ̯ʌlsə]
bedroom	**soveværelse** (i)	['sɒwəˌvæɐ̯ʌlsə]
dining room	**spisestue** (f)	['spiːsəˌstuːə]
living room	**dagligstue** (f)	['dɑwliˌstuːə]
study (home office)	**arbejdsværelse** (i)	['ɑːbɑjdsˌvæɐ̯ʌlsə]
entry room	**entre** (f), **forstue** (f)	[ɑŋ'tʁɛ], ['fɒˌstuːə]
bathroom (room with a bath or shower)	**badeværelse** (i)	['bæːðəˌvæɐ̯ʌlsə]
half bath	**toilet** (i)	[toa'lɛt]
floor	**gulv** (i)	['gɔl]
ceiling	**loft** (i)	['lʌft]
to dust (vt)	**at tørre støv**	[ʌ 'tœɐ̯ʌ 'støˀw]
vacuum cleaner	**støvsuger** (f)	['støwˌsuˀʌ]
to vacuum (vt)	**at støvsuge**	[ʌ 'støwˌsuˀə]
mop	**moppe** (f)	['mʌpə]
dust cloth	**klud** (f)	['kluðˀ]
short broom	**fejekost** (f)	['fɑjəˌkɒst]
dustpan	**fejeblad** (i)	['fɑjəˌblað]
furniture	**møbler** (pl)	['møˀblʌ]

table	bord (i)	['boˀɡ̊]
chair	stol (f)	['stoˀl]
armchair	lænestol (f)	['lɛːnəˌstoˀl]

bookcase	bogskab (i)	['bowˌskæ:b]
shelf	hylde (f)	['hylə]
wardrobe	klædeskab (i)	['klɛ:ðəˌskæˀb]

mirror	spejl (i)	['spɑjˀl]
carpet	tæppe (i)	['tɛpə]
fireplace	pejs (f), kamin (f)	['pɑjˀs], [ka'miˀn]
drapes	gardiner (i pl)	[gɑ'diˀnʌ]
table lamp	bordlampe (f)	['boɡ̊ˌlɑmpə]
chandelier	lysekrone (f)	['lysəˌkʁoːnə]

kitchen	køkken (i)	['køkən]
gas stove (range)	gaskomfur (i)	['gasˌkɔm'fuɡ̊ˀ]
electric stove	elkomfur (i)	['ɛlˌkɔm'fuɡ̊ˀ]
microwave oven	mikroovn (f)	['mikʁoˌɒwˀn]

refrigerator	køleskab (i)	['køːləˌskæˀb]
freezer	fryser (f)	['fʁyːsʌ]
dishwasher	opvaskemaskine (f)	[ʌp'vaskə ma'skiːnə]
faucet	hane (f)	['hæːnə]

meat grinder	kødhakker (f)	['køðˌhɑkʌ]
juicer	juicepresser (f)	['dʒuːsˌpʁasʌ]
toaster	brødrister, toaster (f)	['bʁœðˌʁɛstʌ], ['tɔwstʌ]
mixer	mikser, mixer (f)	['meksʌ]

coffee machine	kaffemaskine (f)	['kɑfə ma'skiːnə]
kettle	kedel (f)	['keðəl]
teapot	tekande (f)	['teˌkanə]

TV set	tv, fjernsyn (i)	['teˀˌveˀ], ['fjæɡ̊nˌsyˀn]
VCR (video recorder)	video (f)	['viˀdjo]
iron (e.g., steam ~)	strygejern (i)	['stʁyəˌjæɡ̊ˀn]
telephone	telefon (f)	[teləˈfoˀn]

15. Professions. Social status

director	direktør (f)	[diɡ̊ek'tøˀɡ̊]
superior	overordnet (f)	['ɒwʌˌɒˀdnəð]
president	præsident (f)	[pʁɛsi'dɛnˀt]
assistant	assistent (f)	[asi'stɛnˀt]
secretary	sekretær (f)	[sekʁə'tɛˀɡ̊]

owner, proprietor	ejer (f)	['ɑjʌ]
partner	partner (f)	['pɑːtnʌ]
stockholder	aktionær (f)	[akɕo'nɛˀɡ̊]

businessman	forretningsmand (f)	[fʌ'ʁatneŋs,man']
millionaire	millionær (f)	[miljo'nɛ'ɐ̯]
billionaire	milliardær (f)	[milja'dɛ'ɐ̯]

actor	skuespiller (f)	['sku:ə,spelʌ]
architect	arkitekt (f)	[ɑki'tɛkt]
banker	bankier (f)	[baŋ'kje]
broker	mægler (f)	['mɛjlʌ]

veterinarian	dyrlæge (f)	['dyɐ̯,lɛ:jə]
doctor	læge (f)	['lɛ:jə]
chambermaid	stuepige (f)	['stuə,pi:ə]
designer	designer (f)	[de'sɑjnʌ]
correspondent	korrespondent (f)	[kɒɒspʌn'dɛn't]
delivery man	bud (i)	['buð]

electrician	elektriker (f)	[e'lɛktʁikʌ]
musician	musiker (f)	['mu'sikʌ]
babysitter	barnepige (f)	['bɑ:nə,pi:ə]
hairdresser	frisør (f)	[fʁi'sø'ɐ̯]
herder, shepherd	hyrde (f)	['hyɐ̯də]

singer (masc.)	sanger (f)	['sɑŋʌ]
translator	oversætter (f)	['ɒwʌ,sɛtʌ]
writer	forfatter (f)	[fʌ'fatʌ]
carpenter	tømrer (f)	['tœmʁʌ]
cook	kok (f)	['kʌk]

fireman	brandmand (f)	['bʁɑn,man]
police officer	politibetjent (f)	[poli'ti be'tjɛn't]
mailman	postbud (i)	['pʌst,buð]
programmer	programmør (f)	[pʁogʁɑ'mø'ɐ̯]
salesman (store staff)	sælger (f)	['sɛljʌ]

worker	arbejder (f)	['ɑ:,bɑj'dʌ]
gardener	gartner (f)	['gɑ:tnʌ]
plumber	blikkenslager (f)	['blekən,slæ'jʌ]

| dentist | tandlæge (f) | ['tan,lɛ:jə] |
| flight attendant (fem.) | stewardesse (f) | [stjuɑ'dɛsə] |

| dancer (masc.) | danser (f) | ['dansʌ] |
| bodyguard | livvagt (f) | ['liw,vagt] |

| scientist | videnskabsmand (f) | ['viðən,skæ'bs man'] |
| schoolteacher | lærer (f) | ['lɛ:ʌ] |

farmer	landmand, bonde (f)	['lan,man'], ['bɔnə]
surgeon	kirurg (f)	[ki'ʁuɐ̯'w]
miner	minearbejder (f)	['mi:nə'ɑ:,bɑj'dʌ]
chef (kitchen chef)	køkkenchef (f)	['køkən,ɕɛ'f]
driver	chauffør (f)	[ɕo'fø'ɐ̯]

16. Sport

kind of sports	idrætsgren (f)	['idʁats͵gʁɛʔn]
soccer	fodbold (f)	['foð͵bʌlʔd]
hockey	ishockey (f)	['is͵hʌki]
basketball	basketball (f)	['baːskət͵bɔːl]
baseball	baseball (f)	['bɛjs͵bɔːl]

volleyball	volleyball (f)	['vʌli͵bɔːl]
boxing	boksning (f)	['bʌksneŋ]
wrestling	brydning (f)	['bʁyðneŋ]
tennis	tennis (f)	['tɛnis]
swimming	svømning (f)	['svœmneŋ]

chess	skak (f)	['skɑk]
running	løb (i)	['løʔb]
athletics	atletik, fri idræt (f)	[atle'tik], ['fʁiʔ 'i͵dʁat]
figure skating	kunstskøjteløb (i)	['kɔnst͵skʌjtelø'b]
cycling	cykelsport (f)	['sykəl͵spɔːt]

billiards	billard (i, f)	['bili͵ɑ'd]
bodybuilding	bodybuilding (f)	['bʌdi͵bilden]
golf	golf (f)	['gʌlʔf]
scuba diving	dykning (f)	['døknen]
sailing	sejlsport (f)	['sɑjl͵spɔːt]
archery	bueskydning (f)	['buːə͵skyðnen]

period, half	halvleg (f)	['ha͵lɑjʔ]
half-time	halvtid (f)	['hal͵tiðʔ]
tie	uafgjorte resultat (i)	['uɑw͵gjoʁʔtə ʁɛsul'tæʔt]
to tie (vi)	at spille uafgjort	[ʌ 'spelə 'uɑw͵gjoʁʔt]

treadmill	løbebånd (i)	['løːbə͵bʌnʔ]
player	spiller (f)	['spelʌ]
substitute	udskiftningsspiller (f)	['uð͵skiftneŋs'spelʌ]
substitutes bench	udskiftningsbænk (f)	['uð͵skiftneŋs͵bɛŋʔk]

match	kamp (f)	['kɑmʔp]
goal	mål (i)	['mɔʔl]
goalkeeper	målmand (f)	['mɔːl͵manʔ]
goal (score)	mål (i)	['mɔʔl]

Olympic Games	de olympiske lege	[di o'lømʔpiskə 'lɑjʔə]
to set a record	at sætte rekord	[ʌ 'sɛtə ʁɛ'kɔːd]
final	finale (f)	[fi'næːlə]
champion	mester (f)	['mɛstʌ]
championship	mesterskab (i)	['mɛstʌ͵skæʔb]

winner	sejrherre (f)	['sɑjʌ͵hæʔʌ]
victory	sejr (f)	['sɑjʔʌ]
to win (vi)	at vinde	[ʌ 'venə]

| to lose (not win) | at tabe | [ʌ 'tæ:bə] |
| medal | medalje (f) | [me'daljə] |

first place	førsteplads (f)	['fœɐ̯stə͵plas]
second place	andenplads (f)	['anən͵plas]
third place	tredjeplads (f)	['tʁɛðjə͵plas]

stadium	stadion (i)	['stæ'djʌn]
fan, supporter	fan (f)	['fæ:n]
trainer, coach	træner (f)	['tʁɛ:nʌ]
training	træning (f)	['tʁɛ:neŋ]

17. Foreign languages. Orthography

language	sprog (i)	['spʁɔ'w]
to study (vt)	at studere	[ʌ stu'de'ʌ]
pronunciation	udtale (f)	['uð͵tæ:lə]
accent	accent (f)	[ak'saŋ]

noun	substantiv (i)	['substan͵tiw']
adjective	adjektiv (i)	['aðjɛk͵tiw']
verb	verbum (i)	['væɐ̯bom]
adverb	adverbium (i)	[að'væɐ̯'bjom]

pronoun	pronomen (i)	[pʁo'no:mən]
interjection	interjektion (f)	[entʌjɛk'ɕo'n]
preposition	præposition (f)	[pʁɛposi'ɕo'n]

root	rod (f)	['ʁo'ð]
ending	endelse (f)	['ɛnəlsə]
prefix	præfiks (i)	[pʁɛ'fiks]
syllable	stavelse (f)	['stæ:vəlsə]
suffix	suffiks (i)	[su'fiks]

stress mark	betoning (f), tryk (i)	[be'to'neŋ], ['tʁœk]
period, dot	punktum (i)	['poŋtɔm]
comma	komma (i)	['kʌma]
colon	kolon (i)	['ko:lʌn]
ellipsis	tre prikker (f pl)	['tʁɛ: 'pʁɛkʌ]

question	spørgsmål (i)	['spœɐ̯s͵mɔ'l]
question mark	spørgsmålstegn (i)	['spœɐ̯s͵mɔls taj'n]
exclamation point	udråbstegn (i)	['uðʁɔbs͵taj'n]

in quotation marks	i anførselstegn	[i 'an͵føɐ̯səls͵taj'n]
in parenthesis	i parentes	[i paɑn'te'əs]
letter	bogstav (i)	['bow͵stæw]
capital letter	stort bogstav (i)	['sto'ɐ̯t 'bogstæw]
sentence	sætning (f)	['sɛtneŋ]
group of words	ordgruppe (f)	['oɐ̯͵gʁupə]

expression	udtryk (i)	['uð,tʁɒɛk]
subject	subjekt (i)	[sub'jɛkt]
predicate	prædikat (i)	[pʁɛdi'kæˀt]
line	linje (f)	['linjə]
paragraph	afsnit (i)	['ɑw,snit]

synonym	synonym (i)	[syno'nyˀm]
antonym	antonym (i)	[anto'nyˀm]
exception	undtagelse (f)	['ɔn,tæˀjəlsə]
to underline (vt)	at understrege	[ʌ 'ɔnʌ,sdʁɑjə]

rules	regler (f pl)	['ʁɛjlʌ]
grammar	grammatik (f)	[gʁɑma'tik]
vocabulary	ordforråd (i)	['oɐ̯fɒ,ʁɔˀð]
phonetics	fonetik (f)	[fonɛ'tik]
alphabet	alfabet (i)	[alfa'beˀt]

textbook	lærebog (f)	['lɛːʌ,bɒˀw]
dictionary	ordbog (f)	['oɐ̯,bɒˀw]
phrasebook	parlør (f)	[pɑ'lœːɐ̯]

word	ord (i)	['oˀɐ̯]
meaning	betydning (f)	[be'tyðˀnen]
memory	hukommelse (f)	[hu'kʌmˀəlsə]

18. The Earth. Geography

the Earth	Jorden	['joˀɐ̯ən]
the globe (the Earth)	jordklode (f)	['joɐ̯,kloːðə]
planet	planet (f)	[pla'neˀt]

geography	geografi (f)	[geogʁɑ'fiˀ]
nature	natur (f)	[na'tuɐ̯ˀ]
map	kort (i)	['kɒːt]
atlas	atlas (i)	['atlas]

in the north	i nord	[i 'noˀɐ̯]
in the south	i syd	[i 'syð]
in the west	i vest	[i 'vɛst]
in the east	i øst	[i 'øst]

sea	hav (i)	['hɑw]
ocean	ocean (i)	[osə'æˀn]
gulf (bay)	bugt (f)	['bɔgt]
straits	stræde (i), sund (i)	['stʁɛːðə], ['sɔnˀ]

continent (mainland)	fastland, kontinent (i)	['fast,lanˀ], [kʌnti'nɛnˀt]
island	ø (f)	['øˀ]
peninsula	halvø (f)	['hal,øˀ]
archipelago	øhav, arkipelag (i)	['ø,hɑw], [ɑkipe'læˀj]

harbor	havn (f)	['hɑw'n]
coral reef	koralrev (i)	[ko'ʁɑlˌʁɛw]
shore	kyst (f)	['køst]
coast	kyst (f)	['køst]

| flow (flood tide) | flod (f) | ['flo'ð] |
| ebb (ebb tide) | ebbe (i) | ['ɛbə] |

latitude	bredde (f)	['bʁɛ'də]
longitude	længde (f)	['lɛŋ'də]
parallel	breddegrad (f)	['bʁɛ'dəˌgʁɑ'ð]
equator	ækvator (f)	[ɛ'kvæːtʌ]

sky	himmel (f)	['heməl]
horizon	horisont (f)	[hɒi'sʌn'ʔt]
atmosphere	atmosfære (f)	[atmo'sfɛːʌ]

mountain	bjerg (i)	['bjæɡ'w]
summit, top	top (f), bjergtop (f)	['tʌp], ['bjæɡwˌtʌp]
cliff	klippe (f)	['klepə]
hill	bakke (f)	['bɑkə]

volcano	vulkan (f)	[vul'kæ'n]
glacier	gletsjer (f)	['glɛtɕʌ]
waterfall	vandfald (i)	['vanˌfal']
plain	slette (f)	['slɛtə]

river	flod (f)	['flo'ð]
spring (natural source)	kilde (f)	['kilə]
bank (of river)	bred (f)	['bʁɛð']
downstream (adv)	nedstrøms	['neðˌstʁœm's]
upstream (adv)	opstrøms	['ʌpˌstʁœm's]

lake	sø (f)	['sø']
dam	dæmning (f)	['dɛmnɛŋ]
canal	kanal (f)	[ka'næ'l]
swamp (marshland)	sump, mose (f)	['sɔm'p], ['moːsə]
ice	is (f)	['i's]

19. Countries of the world. Part 1

Europe	Europa	[œw'ʁoːpa]
European Union	Den Europæiske Union	[dən œwʁo'pɛ'iskə uni'o'n]
European (n)	europæer (f)	[œwʁo'pɛ'ʌ]
European (adj)	europæisk	[œwʁo'pɛ'isk]

Austria	Østrig	['østʁi]
Great Britain	Storbritannien	['stoʁ bʁiˌtaniən]
England	England	['ɛŋ'lan]
Belgium	Belgien	['bɛl'gjən]

Germany	Tyskland	['tysklan²]
Netherlands	Nederlandene	['neːðʌˌlɛnnə]
Holland	Holland	['hʌlan²]
Greece	Grækenland	['gʁɛːkənlan²]
Denmark	Danmark	['dænmɑk]
Ireland	Irland	['iɐlan²]

Iceland	Island	['islan²]
Spain	Spanien	['spæ²njən]
Italy	Italien	[i'tæljən]
Cyprus	Cypern	['kypɒn]
Malta	Malta	['malta]

Norway	Norge	['nɒːw]
Portugal	Portugal	['pɒːtugəl]
Finland	Finland	['fenlan]
France	Frankrig	['fʁɑŋkʁi]
Sweden	Sverige	['svɛʁi²]

Switzerland	Schweiz	['svɑjts]
Scotland	Skotland	['skɒtlan²]
Vatican	Vatikanstaten	['vateˌkæːn 'stæ²tən]
Liechtenstein	Liechtenstein	['liːktənʃtɑjn]
Luxembourg	Luxembourg	['lygsəmˌbɒː]

Monaco	Monaco	[mo'nɑko]
Albania	Albanien	[al'bæ²njən]
Bulgaria	Bulgarien	[bul'gɑːiən]

| Hungary | Ungarn | ['ɔŋgɑ²n] |
| Latvia | Letland | ['lɛtlan²] |

Lithuania	Litauen	['liˌtɑw²ən]
Poland	Polen	['poːlæn]
Romania	Rumænien	[ʁu'mɛ²njən]

| Serbia | Serbien | ['sæɐ̯²biən] |
| Slovakia | Slovakiet | [slova'kiːəð] |

Croatia	Kroatien	[kʁo'æ²tiən]
Czech Republic	Tjekkiet	['tjɛˌkiəð]
Estonia	Estland	['ɛstlan]

| Bosnia and Herzegovina | Bosnien-Herzegovina | ['bosniən hæɐ̯səgo²viːna] |
| Macedonia (Republic of ~) | Makedonien | [mɑkə'doːnjən] |

Slovenia	Slovenien	[slo've:njən]
Montenegro	Montenegro	['mɒntəˌnɛgʁə]
Belarus	Hviderusland	['viːðəˌʁuslan²]
Moldova, Moldavia	Moldova	[mʌl'do²va]
Russia	Rusland	['ʁuslan²]
Ukraine	Ukraine	[ukʁɑ'i²nə]

20. Countries of the world. Part 2

Asia	**Asien**	['æ'ɕən]
Vietnam	**Vietnam**	['vjɛtnɑm]
India	**Indien**	['endjən]
Israel	**Israel**	[isʁɑ:əl]
China	**Kina**	['ki:na]
Lebanon	**Libanon**	['li:banɒn]
Mongolia	**Mongoliet**	[mʌngo'lieð]
Malaysia	**Malaysia**	[ma'lajɕiʌ]
Pakistan	**Pakistan**	['pɑki,stan]
Saudi Arabia	**Saudi-Arabien**	['sawdi ɑ'ʁɑ:bjən]
Thailand	**Thailand**	['tɑjlɛnʔ]
Taiwan	**Taiwan**	['tɑj,væʔn]
Turkey	**Tyrkiet**	[tyɐ̯ki:əð]
Japan	**Japan**	['ja:pæn]
Afghanistan	**Afghanistan**	[ɑw'gæʔni,stan]
Bangladesh	**Bangladesh**	[bɑngla'dɛɕ]
Indonesia	**Indonesien**	[endo'ne:ɕən]
Jordan	**Jordan**	['joɐ̯dan]
Iraq	**Irak**	['iʁɑk]
Iran	**Iran**	['iʁɑn]
Cambodia	**Cambodja**	[kæ:m'boða]
Kuwait	**Kuwait**	[ku'vɑjt]
Laos	**Laos**	['læ:ɒs]
Myanmar	**Myanmar**	[mjanmɐ̯]
Nepal	**Nepal**	['nepalʔ]
United Arab Emirates	**Forenede Arabiske Emirater**	[fʌ'enəðə ɑ'ʁɑʔbiskə emi'ʁɑʔtʌ]
Syria	**Syrien**	['syʁiən]
Palestine	**Palæstina**	[palə'stinɛnə]
South Korea	**Sydkorea**	['syð ko'ʁɛ:a]
North Korea	**Nordkorea**	['noɐ̯ ko'ʁɛ:a]
United States of America	**De Forenede Stater**	[di fʌ'enəðə 'stæʔtʌ]
Canada	**Canada**	['kanæʔda]
Mexico	**Mexiko**	['mɛksiko]
Argentina	**Argentina**	[ɑgɛn'tiʔna]
Brazil	**Brasilien**	[bʁɑ'siljən]
Colombia	**Colombia**	[ko'lɒmbja]
Cuba	**Cuba**	['ku:ba]
Chile	**Chile** (i)	['tji:lə]
Venezuela	**Venezuela**	[venəsu'e:la]
Ecuador	**Ecuador**	[ekwa'doʔɐ̯]
The Bahamas	**Bahamas**	[ba'haʔmas]

Panama	Panama	['panamə]
Egypt	Egypten	[ɛ'gyptən]
Morocco	Marokko	[mɑ'roko]
Tunisia	Tunis	['tu:nis]

Kenya	Kenya	['kɛnja]
Libya	Libyen	['li:bjən]
South Africa	Sydafrika	['syð ˌɑfʁika]
Australia	Australien	[ɑw'stʁɑʔljən]
New Zealand	New Zealand	[nju:'si:lanʔ]

21. Weather. Natural disasters

weather	vejr (i)	['vɛʔɐ̯]
weather forecast	vejrudsigt (f)	['vɛɐ̯ˌuðsegt]
temperature	temperatur (f)	[tɛmpʁɑ'tuɐ̯ʔ]
thermometer	termometer (i)	[tæɐ̯mo'meʔtʌ]
barometer	barometer (i)	[bɑo'meʔtʌ]

sun	sol (f)	['soʔl]
to shine (vi)	at skinne	[ʌ 'skenə]
sunny (day)	solrig	['so:lˌʁiʔ]
to come up (vi)	at stå op	[ʌ stɔʔ 'ʌp]
to set (vi)	at gå ned	[ʌ gɔʔ 'neðʔ]

rain	regn (f)	['ʁɑjʔn]
it's raining	det regner	[de 'ʁɑjnʌ]
pouring rain	øsende regn (f)	['ø:sənə ˌʁɑjʔn]
rain cloud	regnsky (f)	['ʁɑjnˌskyʔ]
puddle	vandpyt (f)	['vanˌpyt]
to get wet (in rain)	at blive våd	[ʌ 'bli:ə 'vɔʔð]

thunderstorm	tordenvejr (i)	['toɐ̯dənˌvɛʔɐ̯]
lightning (~ strike)	lyn (i)	['lyʔn]
to flash (vi)	at glimte	[ʌ 'glemtə]
thunder	torden (f)	['toɐ̯dən]
it's thundering	det tordner	[de 'toɐ̯dnʌ]
hail	hagl (i)	['hɑwʔl]
it's hailing	det hagler	[de 'hɑwlɐ̯]

heat (extreme ~)	hede (f)	['he:ðə]
it's hot	det er hedt	[de 'æɐ̯ 'heðʔ]
it's warm	det er varmt	[de 'æɐ̯ 'vɑʔmt]
it's cold	det er koldt	[de 'æɐ̯ 'kʌlt]

fog (mist)	tåge (f)	['tɔ:wə]
foggy	tåget	['tɔ:wəð]
cloud	sky (f)	['skyʔ]
cloudy (adj)	skyet	['sky:əð]
humidity	fugtighed (f)	['fɔgtiˌheðʔ]

snow	sne (f)	['sne']
it's snowing	det sner	[de 'sne'ʌ]
frost (severe ~, freezing cold)	frost (f)	['fʁʌst]
below zero (adv)	under nul	['ɔnʌ 'nɔl]
hoarfrost	rimfrost (f)	['ʁim‚fʁʌst]

bad weather	uvejr (i)	['u‚vɛ'ɐ̯]
disaster	katastrofe (f)	[kata'stʁo:fə]
flood, inundation	oversvømmelse (f)	['ɒwʌ‚svœm'əlsə]
avalanche	lavine (f)	[la'vi:nə]
earthquake	jordskælv (i)	['joɐ̯‚skɛl'v]

tremor, quake	skælv (i)	['skɛl'v]
epicenter	epicenter (i)	[epi'sɛn'tʌ]
eruption	udbrud (i)	['uð‚bʁuð]
lava	lava (f)	['læ:va]

tornado	tornado (f)	[tɒ'næ:do]
twister	skypumpe (f)	['sky‚pɔmpə]
hurricane	orkan (f)	[ɒ'kæ'n]
tsunami	tsunami (f)	[tsu'nɑ:mi]
cyclone	cyklon (f)	[sy'klo'n]

22. Animals. Part 1

| animal | dyr (i) | ['dyɐ̯'] |
| predator | rovdyr (i) | ['ʁɒw‚dyɐ̯'] |

tiger	tiger (f)	['ti:ʌ]
lion	løve (f)	['lø:və]
wolf	ulv (f)	['ul'v]
fox	ræv (f)	['ʁɛ'w]
jaguar	jaguar (f)	[jagu'ɑ']

lynx	los (f)	['lʌs]
coyote	coyote, prærieulv (f)	[ko'jo:tə], ['pʁɛɐ̯jə‚ul'v]
jackal	sjakal (f)	[ɕa'kæ'l]
hyena	hyæne (f)	[hy'ɛ:nə]

squirrel	egern (i)	['e'jʌn]
hedgehog	pindsvin (i)	['pen‚svi'n]
rabbit	kanin (f)	[ka'ni'n]
raccoon	vaskebjørn (f)	['vaskə‚bjœɐ̯'n]

hamster	hamster (f)	['hɑm'stʌ]
mole	muldvarp (f)	['mul‚vɑ:p]
mouse	mus (f)	['mu's]
rat	rotte (f)	['ʁʌtə]
bat	flagermus (f)	['flɑwʌ‚mu's]

beaver	bæver (f)	['bɛ'vʌ]
horse	hest (f)	['hɛst]
deer	hjort (f)	['jɒːt]
camel	kamel (f)	[ka'me'l]
zebra	zebra (f)	['seːbʁɑ]

whale	hval (f)	['væ'l]
seal	sæl (f)	['sɛ'l]
walrus	hvalros (f)	['val‚ʁʌs]
dolphin	delfin (f)	[dɛl'fi'n]

bear	bjørn (f)	['bjœɐ̯'n]
monkey	abe (f)	['æːbə]
elephant	elefant (f)	[elə'fan't]
rhinoceros	næsehorn (i)	['nɛːsə‚hoɐ̯'n]
giraffe	giraf (f)	[gi'ʁɑf]

hippopotamus	flodhest (f)	['floð‚hɛst]
kangaroo	kænguru (f)	[kɛŋguːʁu]
cat	kat (f)	['kat]
dog	hund (f)	['hun']

cow	ko (f)	['ko']
bull	tyr (f)	['tyɐ̯']
sheep (ewe)	får (i)	['fɑː]
goat	ged (f)	['geð']

donkey	æsel (i)	['ɛ'səl]
pig, hog	svin (i)	['svi'n]
hen (chicken)	høne (f)	['hœːnə]
rooster	hane (f)	['hæːnə]

duck	and (f)	['an']
goose	gås (f)	['gɔ's]
turkey (hen)	kalkun (f)	[kal'ku'n]
sheepdog	hyrdehund (f)	['hyɐ̯də‚hun']

23. Animals. Part 2

bird	fugl (f)	['fu'l]
pigeon	due (f)	['duːə]
sparrow	spurv (f)	['spuɐ̯'w]
tit (great tit)	musvit (f)	[mu'svit]
magpie	skade (f)	['skæːðə]

eagle	ørn (f)	['œɐ̯'n]
hawk	høg (f)	['hø'j]
falcon	falk (f)	['fal'k]
swan	svane (f)	['svæːnə]
crane	trane (f)	['tʁɑːnə]

stork	stork (f)	['stɔːk]
parrot	papegøje (f)	[pɑpe'gʌjə]
peacock	påfugl (f)	['pʌˌfuˀl]
ostrich	struds (f)	['stʁus]

heron	hejre (f)	['hɑjʁʌ]
nightingale	nattergal (f)	['natʌˌgæˀl]
swallow	svale (f)	['svæːlə]
woodpecker	spætte (f)	['spɛtə]
cuckoo	gøg (f)	['gøˀj]
owl	ugle (f)	['uːlə]

penguin	pingvin (f)	[peŋ'viˀn]
tuna	tunfisk (f)	['tuːnˌfesk]
trout	ørred (f)	['œʁʌð]
eel	ål (f)	['ɔˀl]
shark	haj (f)	['hɑjˀ]
crab	krabbe (f)	['kʁabə]
jellyfish	gople, meduse (f)	['gʌplə], [me'duːsə]
octopus	blæksprutte (f)	['blɛkˌspʁutə]

starfish	søstjerne (f)	['søˌstjæɐnə]
sea urchin	søpindsvin (i)	['sø 'penˌsviˀn]
seahorse	søhest (f)	['søˌhɛst]
shrimp	reje (f)	['ʁɑjə]

snake	slange (f)	['slɑŋə]
viper	hugorm (f)	['hɔgˌɔʁˀm]
lizard	firben (i)	['fiʁ'beˀn]
iguana	leguan (f)	[legu'æˀn]
chameleon	kamæleon (f)	[kaməle'oˀn]
scorpion	skorpion (f)	[skɒpi'oˀn]
turtle	skildpadde (f)	['skelˌpaðə]
frog	frø (f)	['fʁœˀ]
crocodile	krokodille (f)	[kʁokə'dilə]

insect, bug	insekt (i)	[en'sɛkt]
butterfly	sommerfugl (f)	['sʌmʌˌfuˀl]
ant	myre (f)	['myːʌ]
fly	flue (f)	['fluːə]

mosquito	stikmyg (f)	['stekˌmyg]
beetle	bille (f)	['bilə]
bee	bi (f)	['biˀ]
spider	edderkop (f)	['ɛðˀʌˌkʌp]

24. Trees. Plants

| tree | træ (i) | ['tʁɛˀ] |
| birch | birk (f) | ['biɐk] |

oak	eg (f)	['e²j]
linden tree	lind (f)	['len²]
aspen	asp (f)	['asp]

maple	løn (f), ahorn (f)	['lœn²], ['a₁hoɐ²n]
spruce	gran (f)	['gʁan]
pine	fyr (f)	['fyɐ²]
cedar	ceder (f)	['se:ðʌ]

poplar	poppel (f)	['pʌpəl]
rowan	røn (f)	['ʁœn²]
beech	bøg (f)	['bø²j]
elm	elm (f)	['ɛl²m]

ash (tree)	ask (f)	['ask]
chestnut	kastanie (i)	[ka'stanjə]
palm tree	palme (f)	['palmə]
bush	busk (f)	['busk]

mushroom	svamp (f)	['svɑm²p]
poisonous mushroom	giftig svamp (f)	['gifti svɑm²p]
cep (Boletus edulis)	karljohan-rørhat (f)	[₁kɑ:ljo'han 'ʁœ²ɐhat]
russula	skørhat (f)	['skøɐ₁hat]
fly agaric	fluesvamp (f)	['flu:ə₁svɑm²p]
death cap	grøn fluesvamp (f)	['gʁœn 'flu:ə₁svɑm²p]

flower	blomst (f)	['blʌm²st]
bouquet (of flowers)	buket (f)	[bu'kɛt]
rose (flower)	rose (f)	['ʁo:sə]
tulip	tulipan (f)	[tuli'pæ²n]
carnation	nellike (f)	['nel²ekə]

camomile	kamille (f)	[ka'milə]
cactus	kaktus (f)	['kɑktus]
lily of the valley	liljekonval (f)	['liljə kɔn'val²]
snowdrop	vintergæk (f)	['ventʌ₁gɛk]
water lily	åkande, nøkkerose (f)	['ɔ²kanə], ['nøkə₁ʁo:sə]

greenhouse (tropical ~)	drivhus (i)	['dʁiw₁hu²s]
lawn	græsplæne (f)	['gʁas₁plɛ:nə]
flowerbed	blomsterbed (i)	['blʌm²stʌ₁beð]

plant	plante (f)	['plantə]
grass	græs (i)	['gʁas]
leaf	blad (i)	['blɑð]
petal	kronblad (i)	['kʁɔn₁blɑð]
stem	stilk (f)	['stel²k]
young plant (shoot)	spire (f)	['spi:ʌ]

cereal crops	kornsorter (f pl)	['koɐn₁sɒ:tʌ]
wheat	hvede (f)	['ve:ðə]
rye	rug (f)	['ʁu²]

oats	havre (f)	['hɑwʁʌ]
millet	hirse (f)	['hiɐ̯sə]
barley	byg (f)	['byg]
corn	majs (f)	['mɑjˀs]
rice	ris (f)	['ʁiˀs]

25. Various useful words

balance (of situation)	balance (f)	[ba'laŋsə]
base (basis)	basis (f)	['bæ:sis]
beginning	begyndelse (f)	[be'gønˀəlsə]
category	kategori (f)	[katəgo'ʁiˀ]

choice	valg (i)	['valˀj]
coincidence	sammenfald (i)	['samənˌfalˀ]
comparison	sammenligning (f)	['samənˌli:neŋ]
degree (extent, amount)	grad (f)	['gʁɑˀð]

development	udvikling (f)	['uðˌvekleŋ]
difference	forskel (f)	['fɔːskɛl]
effect (e.g., of drugs)	effekt (f)	[e'fɛkt]
effort (exertion)	anstrengelse (f)	['anˌstʁaŋˀəlsə]

element	element (i)	[elə'mɛnˀt]
example (illustration)	eksempel (i)	[ɛk'sɛmˀpəl]
fact	faktum (i)	['fɑktɔm]
help	hjælp (f)	['jɛlˀp]

ideal	ideal (i)	[ide'æˀl]
kind (sort, type)	slags (i, f)	['slags]
mistake, error	fejl (f)	['fɑjˀl]
moment	øjeblik (i)	['ʌjəˌblek]

obstacle	hindring (f)	['hendʁɛŋ]
part (~ of sth)	del (f)	['deˀl]
pause (break)	pause (f)	['pɑwsə]
position	position (f)	[posi'çoˀn]

problem	problem (i)	[pʁo'bleˀm]
process	proces (f)	[pʁo'sɛs]
progress	fremskridt (i)	['fʁamˌskʁit]
property (quality)	egenskab (f)	['ejənˌskæˀb]

reaction	reaktion (f)	[ʁɛak'çoˀn]
risk	risiko (f)	['ʁisiko]
secret	hemmelighed (f)	['hɛməliˌheðˀ]
series	serie (f)	['seɐ̯ˀjə]
shape (outer form)	form (f)	['fɔˀm]
situation	situation (f)	[sitwa'çoˀn]

| solution | løsning (f) | ['lø:snen] |
| standard (adj) | standard- | ['stan‚dɑd-] |

stop (pause)	ophold (i)	['ʌp‚hʌlˀ]
style	stil (f)	['stiˀl]
system	system (i)	[sy'steˀm]
table (chart)	tabel (f)	[ta'bɛlˀ]
tempo, rate	tempo (i)	['tɛmpo]

term (word, expression)	term (f)	['tæɐ̯ˀm]
truth (e.g., moment of ~)	sandhed (f)	['san‚heðˀ]
turn (please wait your ~)	tur (f)	['tuɐ̯ˀ]
urgent (adj)	haster	['hastə]

utility (usefulness)	nytte (f)	['nøtə]
variant (alternative)	variant (f)	[vɑi'anˀt]
way (means, method)	måde (f)	['mɔ:ðə]
zone	zone (f)	['so:nə]

26. Modifiers. Adjectives. Part 1

additional (adj)	yderligere	['yðʌ‚liˀʌʌ]
ancient (~ civilization)	oldtids-	['ʌl‚tiðs-]
artificial (adj)	kunstig	['kɔnsti]
bad (adj)	dårlig	['dɔ:li]
beautiful (person)	smuk	['smɔk]

big (in size)	stor	['stoˀɐ̯]
bitter (taste)	bitter	['betʌ]
blind (sightless)	blind	['blenˀ]
central (adj)	central	[sɛn'tʁɑˀl]

children's (adj)	børne-	['bœɐ̯nə-]
clandestine (secret)	hemmelig	['hɛməli]
clean (free from dirt)	ren	['ʁɛˀn]
clever (smart)	klog	['klɔˀw]
compatible (adj)	forenelig	[fʌ'eˀnəli]

contented (satisfied)	tilfreds	[te'fʁɛs]
dangerous (adj)	farlig	['fɑ:li]
dead (not alive)	død	['døðˀ]
dense (fog, smoke)	tæt	['tɛt]
difficult (decision)	svær	['svɛˀɐ̯]

dirty (not clean)	snavset	['snɑwsəð]
easy (not difficult)	let	['lɛt]
empty (glass, room)	tom	['tʌmˀ]
exact (amount)	eksakt, præcis	[ɛk'sɑkt], [pʁɛ'siˀs]
excellent (adj)	udmærket	['uð‚mæɐ̯kəð]
excessive (adj)	overdreven	['ɔwʌ‚dʁɛˀvən]

exterior (adj)	**ydre**	['yðʁʌ]
fast (quick)	**hurtig**	['hoɐ̯ti]
fertile (land, soil)	**frugtbar**	['fʁɔgtˌbɑ']
fragile (china, glass)	**skør**	['skø'ɐ̯]
free (at no cost)	**gratis**	['gʁɑ:tis]
fresh (~ water)	**ferske**	['fæɐ̯skə]
frozen (food)	**frossen**	['fʁɔsən]
full (completely filled)	**fuld**	['ful']
happy (adj)	**lykkelig**	['løkəli]
hard (not soft)	**hård**	['hɔ']
huge (adj)	**enorm**	[e'nɒ'm]
ill (sick, unwell)	**syg**	['sy']
immobile (adj)	**ubevægelig**	[ube'vɛ'jəli]
important (adj)	**vigtig**	['vegti]
interior (adj)	**indre**	['endʁʌ]
last (e.g., ~ week)	**forrige**	['fɒ:iə]
last (final)	**sidste**	['sistə]
left (e.g., ~ side)	**venstre**	['vɛnstʁʌ]
legal (legitimate)	**lovlig**	['lɒwli]
light (in weight)	**let**	['lɛt]
liquid (fluid)	**flydende**	['fly:ðənə]
long (e.g., ~ hair)	**lang**	['lɑŋ']
loud (voice, etc.)	**høj**	['hʌj']
low (voice)	**lav**	['læ'v]

27. Modifiers. Adjectives. Part 2

main (principal)	**hoved-**	['ho:əð-]
matt, matte	**mat**	['mat]
mysterious (adj)	**mystisk**	['mystisk]
narrow (street, etc.)	**smal**	['smal']
native (~ country)	**hjem-**	['jɛm'-]
negative (~ response)	**negativ**	['negaˌtiw']
new (adj)	**ny**	['ny']
next (e.g., ~ week)	**næste**	['nɛstə]
normal (adj)	**normal**	[nɒ'mæ'l]
not difficult (adj)	**let**	['lɛt]
obligatory (adj)	**obligatorisk**	[obliga'to'ɐ̯isk]
old (house)	**gammel**	['gaməl]
open (adj)	**åben**	['ɔ:bən]
opposite (adj)	**modsat**	['moðˌsat]
ordinary (usual)	**almindelig**	[al'men'li]
original (unusual)	**original**	[ɒigi'næ'l]
personal (adj)	**personlig**	[pæɐ̯'so'nli]

polite (adj)	høflig	['høfli]
poor (not rich)	fattig	['fati]

possible (adj)	mulig	['muːli]
principal (main)	hoved-	['hoːəð-]
probable (adj)	sandsynlig	[san'syˀnli]
prolonged (e.g., ~ applause)	langvarig	['laŋˌvaˀi]
public (open to all)	offentlig	['ʌfəntli]

rare (adj)	sjælden	['ɕɛlən]
raw (uncooked)	rå	['ʁɔˀ]
right (not left)	højre	['hʌjʁʌ]
ripe (fruit)	moden	['moˀðən]

risky (adj)	risikabel	[ʁisiˈkæˀbəl]
sad (~ look)	trist	['tʁist]
second hand (adj)	brugt	['bʁɔgt]
shallow (water)	grund	['gʁɔnˀ]
sharp (blade, etc.)	skarp	['skɑːp]

short (in length)	kort	['kɒːt]
similar (adj)	lignende	['liːnənə]
small (in size)	lille	['lilə]
smooth (surface)	glat	['glat]
soft (~ toys)	blød	['bløˀð]

solid (~ wall)	solid, holdbar	[so'liðˀ], ['hʌlˌbɑˀ]
sour (flavor, taste)	sur	['suʁˀ]
spacious (house, etc.)	rummelig	['ʁɔməli]
special (adj)	speciel	[spe'ɕɛlˀ]

straight (line, road)	lige	['liːə]
strong (person)	stærk	['stæʁk]
stupid (foolish)	dum	['dɔmˀ]
superb, perfect (adj)	udmærket	['uðˌmæʁkəð]

sweet (sugary)	sød	['søðˀ]
tan (adj)	solbrændt	['soːlˌbʁanˀt]
tasty (delicious)	lækker	['lɛkʌ]
unclear (adj)	uklar	['uˌklɑˀ]

28. Verbs. Part 1

to accuse (vt)	at anklage	[ʌ 'anˌklæˀjə]
to agree (say yes)	at samtykke	[ʌ 'samˌtykə]
to announce (vt)	at meddele	[ʌ 'mɛðˌdeˀlə]
to answer (vi, vt)	at svare	[ʌ 'svaːɑ]
to apologize (vi)	at undskylde sig	[ʌ 'ɔnˌskylˀə saj]
to arrive (vi)	at ankomme	[ʌ 'anˌkʌmˀə]

to ask (~ oneself)	at spørge	[ʌ 'spœɐ̯ʌ]
to be absent	at være fraværende	[ʌ 'vɛ:ʌ 'fʁɑˌvɛˀʌnə]
to be afraid	at frygte	[ʌ 'fʁœgtə]
to be born	at fødes	[ʌ 'fø:ðəs]

to be in a hurry	at skynde sig	[ʌ 'skønə saj]
to beat (to hit)	at slå	[ʌ 'slɔˀ]
to begin (vt)	at begynde	[ʌ be'gønˀə]
to believe (in God)	at tro	[ʌ 'tʁoˀ]
to belong to ...	at tilhøre ...	[ʌ 'telˌhøˀʌ ...]
to break (split into pieces)	at bryde	[ʌ 'bʁy:ðə]

to build (vt)	at bygge	[ʌ 'bygə]
to buy (purchase)	at købe	[ʌ 'kø:bə]
can (v aux)	at kunne	[ʌ 'kunə]
can (v aux)	at kunne	[ʌ 'kunə]
to cancel (call off)	at aflyse, at annullere	[ʌ 'awˌlyˀsə], [ʌ anu'leˀʌ]

to catch (vt)	at fange	[ʌ 'faŋə]
to change (vt)	at ændre	[ʌ 'ɛndʁʌ]
to check (to examine)	at tjekke	[ʌ 'tjɛkə]
to choose (select)	at vælge	[ʌ 'vɛljə]
to clean up (tidy)	at rydde op	[ʌ 'ʁyðə ʌp]
to close (vt)	at lukke	[ʌ 'lɔkə]
to compare (vt)	at sammenligne	[ʌ 'samənˌliˀnə]
to complain (vi, vt)	at klage	[ʌ 'klæ:jə]
to confirm (vt)	at bekræfte	[ʌ be'kʁaftə]
to congratulate (vt)	at gratulere	[ʌ gʁatu'leˀʌ]

to cook (dinner)	at lave	[ʌ 'læ:və]
to copy (vt)	at kopiere	[ʌ ko'pjeˀʌ]
to cost (vt)	at koste	[ʌ 'kʌstə]
to count (add up)	at tælle	[ʌ 'tɛlə]
to count on ...	at regne med ...	[ʌ 'ʁajnə mɛ ...]

to create (vt)	at oprette, at skabe	[ʌ 'ʌbˌʁatə], [ʌ 'skæ:bə]
to cry (weep)	at græde	[ʌ 'gʁa:ðə]
to dance (vi, vt)	at danse	[ʌ 'dansə]
to deceive (vi, vt)	at snyde	[ʌ 'sny:ðə]
to decide (~ to do sth)	at beslutte	[ʌ be'slutə]

to delete (vt)	at slette, at fjerne	[ʌ 'slɛtə], [ʌ 'fjæɐ̯nə]
to demand (request firmly)	at kræve	[ʌ 'kʁɛ:və]
to deny (vt)	at fornægte *	[ʌ fʌ'nɛgtə]
to depend on ...	at afhænge af ...	[ʌ 'awˌhɛŋˀə a ...]
to despise (vt)	at foragte	[ʌ fʌ'agtə]

to die (vi)	at dø	[ʌ 'døˀ]
to dig (vt)	at grave	[ʌ 'gʁa:və]
to disappear (vi)	at forsvinde	[ʌ fʌ'svenˀə]
to discuss (vt)	at diskutere	[ʌ disku'teˀʌ]
to disturb (vt)	at forstyrre	[ʌ fʌ'styɐ̯ˀʌ]

29. Verbs. Part 2

to dive (vi)	at dykke	[ʌ 'døkə]
to divorce (vi)	at blive skilt	[ʌ 'bliːə 'skelˀt]
to do (vt)	at gøre	[ʌ 'gœːʌ]
to doubt (have doubts)	at tvivle	[ʌ 'tviwlə]
to drink (vi, vt)	at drikke	[ʌ 'dʁɛkə]
to drop (let fall)	at tabe	[ʌ 'tæːbə]
to dry (clothes, hair)	at tørre	[ʌ 'tœɐ̯ʌ]
to eat (vi, vt)	at spise	[ʌ 'spiːsə]
to end (~ a relationship)	at afbryde	[ʌ 'ɑwˌbʁyˀðə]
to excuse (forgive)	at undskylde	[ʌ 'ɔnˌskylˀə]
to exist (vi)	at eksistere	[ʌ ɛksi'steˀʌ]
to expect (foresee)	at forudse	[ʌ 'fɒuðˌseˀ]
to explain (vt)	at forklare	[ʌ fʌ'klɑˀɑ]
to fall (vi)	at falde	[ʌ 'falə]
to fight (street fight, etc.)	at slås	[ʌ 'slʌs]
to find (vt)	at finde	[ʌ 'fenə]
to finish (vt)	at slutte	[ʌ 'slutə]
to fly (vi)	at flyve	[ʌ 'flyːvə]
to forbid (vt)	at forbyde	[ʌ fʌ'byˀðə]
to forget (vi, vt)	at glemme	[ʌ 'glɛmə]
to forgive (vt)	at tilgive	[ʌ 'telˌgiˀ]
to get tired	at blive træt	[ʌ 'bliːə 'tʁat]
to give (vt)	at give	[ʌ 'giˀ]
to go (on foot)	at gå	[ʌ 'gɔˀ]
to hate (vt)	at hade	[ʌ 'hæːðə]
to have (vt)	at have	[ʌ 'hæːvə]
to have breakfast	at spise morgenmad	[ʌ 'spiːsə 'mɒːɒnˌmað]
to have dinner	at spise aftensmad	[ʌ 'spiːsə 'ɑftənsˌmað]
to have lunch	at spise frokost	[ʌ 'spiːsə 'fʁɔkʌst]
to hear (vt)	at høre	[ʌ 'høːʌ]
to help (vt)	at hjælpe	[ʌ 'jɛlpə]
to hide (vt)	at gemme	[ʌ 'gɛmə]
to hope (vi, vt)	at håbe	[ʌ 'hɔːbə]
to hunt (vi, vt)	at jage	[ʌ 'jæːjə]
to hurry (vi)	at skynde sig	[ʌ 'skønə sɑj]
to insist (vi, vt)	at insistere	[ʌ ensi'steˀʌ]
to insult (vt)	at fornærme	[ʌ fʌ'næɐ̯'mə]
to invite (vt)	at indbyde, at invitere	[ʌ 'enˌbyˀðə], [ʌ envi'teˀʌ]
to joke (vi)	at spøge	[ʌ 'spøːjə]
to keep (vt)	at beholde	[ʌ be'hʌlˀə]
to kill (vt)	at dræbe, at myrde	[ʌ 'dʁɛːbə], [ʌ 'myɐ̯də]
to know (sb)	at kende	[ʌ 'kɛnə]

to know (sth)	at vide	[ʌ 'viːðə]
to like (I like ...)	at kunne lide	[ʌ 'kunə 'liːðə]
to look at ...	at se på ...	[ʌ 'seˀ pɔˀ ...]

to lose (umbrella, etc.)	at tabe, at miste	[ʌ 'tæːbə], [ʌ 'mestə]
to love (sb)	at elske	[ʌ 'ɛlskə]
to make a mistake	at tage fejl	[ʌ 'tæˀ fɑjˀl]
to meet (vi, vt)	at mødes	[ʌ 'møːðəs]
to miss (school, etc.)	at forsømme	[ʌ fʌ'sœmˀə]

30. Verbs. Part 3

to obey (vi, vt)	at underordne sig	[ʌ 'ɔnʌˌɒˀdnə sɑj]
to open (vt)	at åbne	[ʌ 'ɔːbnə]
to participate (vi)	at deltage	[ʌ 'delˌtæˀ]
to pay (vi, vt)	at betale	[ʌ be'tæˀlə]
to permit (vt)	at tillade	[ʌ 'teˌlæˀðə]

to play (children)	at lege	[ʌ 'lɑjə]
to pray (vi, vt)	at bede	[ʌ 'beˀðə]
to promise (vt)	at love	[ʌ 'lɔːvə]
to propose (vt)	at foreslå	[ʌ 'fɔːɒˌslɔˀ]
to prove (vt)	at bevise	[ʌ be'viˀsə]
to read (vi, vt)	at læse	[ʌ 'lɛːsə]

to receive (vt)	at modtage	[ʌ 'moðˌtæˀ]
to rent (sth from sb)	at leje	[ʌ 'lɑjə]
to repeat (say again)	at gentage	[ʌ 'gɛnˌtæˀ]
to reserve, to book	at reservere	[ʌ ʁɛsæɡ'veˀʌ]
to run (vi)	at løbe	[ʌ 'løːbə]

to save (rescue)	at redde	[ʌ 'ʁɛðə]
to say (~ thank you)	at sige	[ʌ 'siː]
to see (vt)	at se	[ʌ 'seˀ]
to sell (vt)	at sælge	[ʌ 'sɛljə]
to send (vt)	at sende	[ʌ 'sɛnə]
to shoot (vi)	at skyde	[ʌ 'skyːðə]

to shout (vi)	at skrige	[ʌ 'skʁiːə]
to show (vt)	at vise	[ʌ 'viːsə]
to sign (document)	at underskrive	[ʌ 'ɔnʌˌskʁiˀvə]
to sing (vi)	at synge	[ʌ 'søŋə]
to sit down (vi)	at sætte sig	[ʌ 'sɛtə sɑj]

to smile (vi)	at smile	[ʌ 'smiːlə]
to speak (vi, vt)	at tale	[ʌ 'tæːlə]
to steal (money, etc.)	at stjæle	[ʌ 'stjɛːlə]
to stop (please ~ calling me)	at stoppe, at slutte	[ʌ 'stʌpə], [ʌ 'slutə]
to study (vt)	at studere	[ʌ stu'deˀʌ]

to swim (vi)	at svømme	[ʌ 'svœmə]
to take (vt)	at tage	[ʌ 'tæˀ]
to talk to ...	at tale med ...	[ʌ 'tæːlə mɛ ...]
to tell (story, joke)	at fortælle	[ʌ fʌ'tɛlˀə]
to thank (vt)	at takke	[ʌ 'tɑkə]
to think (vi, vt)	at tænke	[ʌ 'tɛŋkə]

to translate (vt)	at oversætte	[ʌ 'ɒwʌˌsɛtə]
to trust (vt)	at stole på	[ʌ 'stoːlə pɔˀ]
to try (attempt)	at forsøge	[ʌ fʌ'søˀjə]
to turn (e.g., ~ left)	at svinge	[ʌ 'svɛŋə]
to turn off	at slukke	[ʌ 'slɔkə]

to turn on	at tænde	[ʌ 'tɛnə]
to understand (vt)	at forstå	[ʌ fʌ'stɔˀ]
to wait (vt)	at vente	[ʌ 'vɛntə]
to want (wish, desire)	at ville	[ʌ 'vilə]
to work (vi)	at arbejde	[ʌ 'ɑːˌbɑjˀdə]
to write (vt)	at skrive	[ʌ 'skʁiːvə]

www.ingramcontent.com/pod-product-compliance
Lightning Source LLC
Chambersburg PA
CBHW060024050426
42448CB00012B/2866